C000314637

50
years
on the
water

EDITED BY

PETER SANDBACH

Designed & Produced by The Printing House Ltd 01270 212100

Contents

Appendices

Foreword

Dear fellow members, I am lucky to be the President of this great Class Association at this time. I am privileged to have met and made friends with so many wonderful and genuine people in the Class during social and sailing events at home and abroad. Open arms were extended to me and to members of my family in the homes of fellow members. The sport of sailing is appreciated and sailing in GP14's is the common bond that fosters such friendship and friendliness.

We owe a debt to the late and great Jack Holt that can only be repaid by our acknowledgement of his genius in designing a boat that is so adaptable that it satisfies the needs of "The Do It Yourself" enthusiast, the racing members and eases the cost concerns of all boat owners by easing the cost in the market place.

The position of the Class in the world of sailing depended to a great extent on the articles of the Constitution and the adherence to the Rules. The binding element was the calibre of the Officers and Committee members who gave unstintingly of their time, efforts and expertise in administering the business of the Association combined with dealing with the concerns of the GP14 sailors. Their efforts were appreciated and rewarded through the spreading of the CLASS throughout the World. (The Class Handbook shows all.) With that Diaspora came lines of communication, friendly contacts and valued friendships.

I must pay tribute to other agencies who helped hugely in giving the Class an enviable position in the world of sailing. The builders of boats, providers of sails, the suppliers of spars and rigging and the host clubs who adopted the Class, provided racing and sailing facilities and hosted events at club, local, area, national and international levels. Through their combined efforts we enjoy our sport at attractive venues, and sail and race in beautiful boats with absolute confidence in the respective organising authorities. Nor am I forgetting the many members of the Class who have been and are involved in the sport at national and international administrative levels. The most recent World Championship sailed at Durban, South Africa, hosted by Point Bay Y.C., organised by the South African GP14 Class Association and enjoyed hugely by all who were involved on and off the water. For me, this enjoyed experience encapsulates all that our Association means to each of our members.

On your behalf I wish to thank most sincerely all who have contributed to this history of the GP14 Class International Association and to pay tribute to my friend and fellow member Mr Peter Sandbach for whom this work has been a labour of love.

Kindest regards and enjoyable reading.

Riocard O'Tiarnaigh
President

From the Chairman
of the Royal Yachting Association

MR.K.ELLIS

PATRON Her Majesty The Queen
PRESIDENT The Princess Royal KG, GCVO

Royal Yachting Association

The GP Class has been steered, with great success, through all the problems that beset the development of a national institution. It's the people of the Class that have really formed the boat over the past fifty years. The book is an account of the Class by those who sailed in it and those who administered the Association.

Jack Holt was my idol, with Ian Proctor, he was instrumental in reforming my home club after the Second World War. When I started sailing as a cadet the legend of Jack Holt, the helmsman and the revolutionary dinghy designer was well established.

All the designs from his board had their first real trial, in secret, at the Aldenham Sailing Club at Elstree, my home club. Can you imagine, an un-named 14 foot prototype with flat sides at the home, as it was then, of one of the premiere Merlin Rocket clubs in the country?

In 1975 I became Chairman of the RYA Centreboard Committee with Jack Holt as Technical Adviser. For twelve years we worked on many National Classes as they developed, but he never failed to mention the 'Independent' GP14 at our meetings.

At the ISAF meeting in Sydney in November 1999 I was delighted to support the recommendation that the GP14 should become an International Classic Class.

This book represents an excellent commemoration of the development of the GP14 over the past fifty years. It's very important that the sailing world knows and understands of the contribution made by the Class in the development of dinghy sailing.

Best Wishes

Ken Ellis

Introduction

In producing this book we have tried to do two things. To entertain you by recalling memories for those of you who knew the earlier days of the Class, perhaps sailing in GP's in the 50's, or if you are a more recent member, give you an idea of the background which has led this Class to such great strengths. We have also tried to provide a more detailed history of the Class and boat than has been possible in the past.

The chapters have been written by a diverse cross section of our membership. Some are reprints of articles previously published. They all have a place in the record which has defined a culture that has grown in strength continuously since the launch of the first fleet of GP14's at Aberdovey in 1950. This culture, built round friendship and fellowship, has engendered a loyalty to the Class which is second to none in the sailing world. A saying first heard many many years ago "We joined for the boat but stayed for the people," is as true today as it was then.

We do thank the many contributors to this book. They reflect past and present views. In such circumstances, it is difficult to avoid repeating a memory of an event or a person. To edit individuals' views would spoil their contribution. We hope that where there may be slight contradictions it may be seen as a product of our 50 years and not too serious.

Peter Sandbach.
1984-1992 Association Secretary

How it Started

Your new *Editor has asked me to cast my mind back over 20 years and write a few lines, mainly for the benefit of new members, on how the Association was formed. With such a poor memory as mine, this is asking a great deal, so, should a few facts be astray, I beg forgiveness

In the late-forties, the Dovey Sailing Club was formed. One of its first briefs was to acquire a one design sailing dinghy suitable for estuary and sea sailing. It should also be one which could be built professionally or from a set of plans by anyone who could read or write. After much time and deliberation aligned to the persuasive qualities of the late Dusty Pollock of Bell Woodworking Co. Ltd. the club chose the G.P. Fourteen.

The launch of GP No. 1 (reproduced from Cine Film)

Accordingly, the prototype was built and arrived in Aberdovey towards the end of 1949. The locals were aghast with pain at what they saw, a plywood boat - and their comments varied from "It will not float" to "It will capsize as soon as the sails fill" - "Bound to, it has a wooden centre board". However, a boat was launched and came fully up to expectations - it was a day to be remembered - wind force 0 - strong ebb tide - lovely sunshine - conditions ideal for a prototype! Ten were duly ordered and so the GP was born.

It was obvious to those of us who knew a little about sailing that we were on to a winner - it had floated, it had not capsized and the plywood had stood up to all asked of it! However, the Dovey estuary proved a tough testing ground, the boat exceeded all expectations - its good qualities were evident and soon clubs from far afield were sending representatives to sail the boat.

During 1950/51 at least ten clubs adopted the GP, not only in Wales but as far afield as the Hamble River and Windermere. Accordingly, it was decided to form an Owners' Association and the first official meeting was at the residence of Dr. Ryle who then lived at Drapers Hall, Shrewsbury.

About twenty enthusiastic GP owners turned up that cold, foggy, November's evening (11th November 1951). Who present could ever forget those hours spent drinking tea and swapping yarns?, and, in between, the GP14 Class Association was born.

Drapers Hall, Shrewsbury

One of the main topics of discussion was whether it should be the "Bell" Class or GP Fourteen; the vote was close but G.P. Fourteen it was - the General Purpose gimmick carried the day.

The meeting also decided to draw up rules, plan a National Championship and discussed a whole range of topics relating to the boat.

The annual subscription was fixed at 5/- and the meeting ended with all present sworn to sell the boat - which they did - not too difficult a task as it was outstanding value for money, even in those days, as my receipt for £98.10.0d. clearly shows.

The first meeting's minutes

Much water has passed down the Dovey since then but last week, twenty three years later practically to the day, I re-visited the scene of that initial launching - it made me think - then there was one, today there are over 10,000

"The past is but story told, may the future be writ in gold"

Ed. On June 17th. 2000 the Dovey Yacht Club celebrated the 50th. Anniversary of its founding. As a great honour to the GP14 Class, it had postponed the actual day so that it might coincide with the 50th. anniversary of the launching of the first GP to arrive in Aberdovey. It was an honour to be there, thank you. Dovey Y.C.
By E. Howard-Davies
*Reprinted from Mainsail

The GP14 Class

I have always loved boats and the sea. I owe it to my father who first took me sailing at about the age of five, so it was not to be wondered at that, under his somewhat austere but kindly eye, I grew up a proficient yacht hand. He was a good seaman having, in his early life, gone to sea before the mast. As a result, I reaped handsome benefits and knotting, lashing and splicing became second nature. I could tie a bowline behind my back in the dark and, as a spin off, I have always been able to tie up a parcel in the sure knowledge that it would not come undone. It is in such ways that the seaman has the edge over the landsman.

Rowing and dinghy work came as naturally as riding a bicycle. My cup of happiness overflowed when a sailing dinghy with a lug sail was added to the fleet. We had no outboard motors in those days and I was ready, at the drop of a hat, to bring aboard a guest, under sail or oars, to go ashore for the milk or to collect the mail. It is thus one really learns to handle a small sailing boat.

Swimming I learned in a school swimming bath. There is no better way of learning and the younger the better. I was lucky to have a games master who could really teach swimming and, thanks to him, I have always been at home in the water.

Were it not for my father's love of the sea and my early introduction to it, I should have missed much in life. To me it is difficult to visualise existence against a non-nautical background. Sailing small boats develops, particularly in the young, a resourcefulness and confidence not acquired in any other way because once connection with the land is severed the skipper of a vessel, however small, has to cope with the elemental forces of the wind, the waves and the tides. GP14 parents can do the same for their children.

Many have expressed their gratitude to me- they too owe something to my father and to others, from whom I learned about the sea. For instance, Bill and Dick Clements, (Cockney brothers), were skipper and mate of my father's Thames barge, Daisy, taught me, among many things, to handle sails the size of a tennis court; to bring a 170 ton barge alongside in a dock so that she wouldn't crush "a heggshell" under topsail alone.

Well, 1 suppose you will wonder what all these autobiographical details have to do with the conception of boats like the Cadet and the GP14 but I am sure that with anything to do with the sea there is no substitute for practical experience and that is how I got it.

After thirty years, two major wars and several minor scraps, the end of Hitler's war came. I knew, from experience, that the "run-down" would be a frightful bore. I might even become an Air Commodore! — so I decided to leave the service. During my whole career, in various parts of the world, I had somehow managed to maintain a boat or yacht of some kind, a lateen rigged Felucca in Egypt, a motor boat on the Tigris at Baghdad.

One evening at a cocktail party, I was talking to a rather tired, charming man who said he was a publisher. He was the Chairman of Iliffes, publishers of Yachting World. On learning that, as a yachtsman, I had read the magazine, he asked whether I could write because he was looking for an editor. He, himself, had kept the journal going during the war, but no longer had the time. Would I like the job? Rather grudgingly I agreed to think about it because I thought it a lousy magazine, and said so. Instead of taking umbrage, he seemed delighted and promised to give me a free hand and no interference. After giving it a week or two's thought, I went to the office, asked which was the Editor's chair, and to the surprise of the staff, one man and a typist, sat in it. There, I remained for the next sixteen years. From then on, Yachting World had a mission — to get people afloat, especially those with slender means. Robert Clark designed me the Yachting World 5 tonner, a beautiful small yacht, followed by Arthur Robb's Jenny Wren, a lovely little mottle motor cruiser.

Then I fell in with the Merlin Syndicate, trying to produce a 14 ft. racing dinghy at a reasonable price. The 14 ft. International had become so expensive as to be beyond the reach of most young helmsmen. The Merlin Class was duly launched and from that exercise I learned a great deal about racing dinghies and the people who sailed them, how to manage a Class and so on.

At the back of my mind I had always planned to start a racing Class for the young. Just before the war I had built a small hard chine, flat snout slab-sided boat for my young to sail. It was much like the Cadet. The advent of marine ply which, unlike timber, was easy to bend, gave me the idea beginning with the Cadet, of the Build-Her-Yourself boats. A youngster could buy a set of plans or a set of parts, build his own boat and win a race in her. She could also be built by dad in the spare bedroom (and launched through the window), the drawing room or garage or at school carpentry classes.

I had become associated with Jack Holt through the Merlin Class, so I naturally turned to him for a design. After many explanations and rough sketches I knew 1 had found the right man. The result was the Cadet. We built a prototype which was sailed, and of course criticised by, the Merlin Syndicate, but the only alteration was to fill out the forward end of the hull a little, to be certain that, when running, especially when carrying a spinnaker, she would not bury her bow, a common fault in so many small sailing boats. Today, twenty four years later, the Cadet is sailed all over the world. The only alteration has been to give her a larger spinnaker.

My next concern was for the family man. So many young marrieds' had looked wistfully at Merlins. And sadly, with their wife and a couple of kids walked away. The Build-Her-Yourself concept having been successfully demonstrated and established by the Cadet, was obviously right for a bigger boat. So many young married men have been tied down to spades and buckets on the beach simply because there was no alternative. The young family could swim, but they too were becoming bored. Bathing and sand castles were becoming kid's stuff. If dad went off racing at weekends, mum would get bored sitting at home or on the beach with the kids, so, I evolved in my mind a boat which could be raced by dad (and mum, perhaps) on Saturday and used to take the family picnicking on Sunday, and vice versa. It had to carry two adults and two or three children, in safety. It must be possible for the family to sit in the boat, but for dad to sit out on the side deck when racing.

Yachting World
G.P. Fourteen

HOW TO BUILD FROM "YACHTING WORLD" PLANS

By Michael Verney

PART I

ALL working drawings for yachts appear rather complex when first viewed by the prospective amateur builder. Therefore, before starting any constructional work one should spend several hours studying the drawings and checking each part from one drawing to the other so that an accurate impression of the whole structure is imprinted upon the mind.

The *Yachting World* G.P. Fourteen has been specially designed for amateur building by Jack Holt, who also designed the highly successful *Yachting World* Cadet. The five sheets of working drawings have been prepared as clear and straightforward as they could be. With the aid of the details to be given in these three articles it should be quite easy for any enthusiast to complete a successful craft.

There is really no need to lay down any of the lines full size on the floor, as for almost all round bilge designs. All the frames and also the stem and transom are drawn out to full size on Sheets 3, 4 and 5 of the drawings. The amateur has only to mark his timber from these drawings to obtain a really accurate framing.

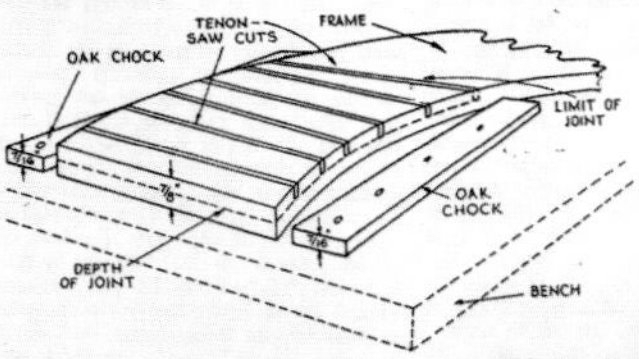

tion on Sheet 3. In most cases these dimensions can be used as an actual timber order but some parts must be measured off the drawings in one direction.

Each frame consists of three pieces, two up each of the topsides and one right across the bottom. The two joints at the chines of each frame are formed by halving the parts into each other and securing with wood screws until the resin glue hardens. These wood screws are not shown on the drawing as they are quite arbitrary in size and number but generally speaking, ¾in No. 8 brass screws will suffice, and these should be left in after glueing. Care must be taken that these screws are not in the way of the 2in screws which secure the chines to the frames.

Each part of each frame should be marked from the patterns by resting them underneath the sheet of hardboard and driving fine panel pins through at all points of interest. These points include each corner of the timber, the outlines of the notches for chines, stringers, gunwales and limber holes, and also the line where the halved joint cuts the adjacent frame member.

However, these patterns should not be used direct from the paper to the wood, or certain errors are bound to creep in. Instead, Sheets 4 and 5, and preferably the part of Sheet 3 showing the outline of the stem, should be gummed on to sheets of hardboard or thin plywood. Masonite ⅛in thick would be admirable, costing sevenpence a square foot. These sheets can be used afterwards for other purposes although there will be small holes in them, caused by marking through.

The sizes of timber for each part of the frames are listed in the specifica-

It will be observed that the frames are extended to form legs which rest on the floor when the hull is erected upside-down ready for planking. In this way the usual elaborate arrangement of stocks used for erecting the framework is eliminated and the

extra leg pieces are sawn off after the hull is turned over.

The amateur may find some difficulty in cutting out the halved joints where the topside and bottom parts of the frames meet. This halving is most readily achieved by resting the ends of each part in turn in a rough jig as shown in Fig. 1. As the mahogany used for the frames is ⅜in thick, the chocks of the jig must be ⅜in thick. A tenon saw is then used to make numerous cuts in one direction across the joint, each cut being just half way through the wood, so that the saw teeth just rest evenly upon the jig at each end. Afterwards the frame piece must be removed from the jig and chiselled out until all the wood down to the depth of the saw-cuts has been pared away to an even surface. These joints in the frames can be seen in the photograph, Fig. 2. Resin glue should be used, and it is imperative that a really strong bond is obtained because the large screws holding the chines to the frames have to pass right through these joints for the whole length of the screws.

Before the frames are glued permanently they should each be rested upon the pattern to check the accuracy of the joints, and any alterations carried out. After glueing, each frame should again be rested upon the pattern to check the accuracy of the notches. These must be exactly as shown on the drawings. It will be realized that there is bevel on the edges of almost all the frame

Fig. 1

Fig. 2

She must be so designed that she could be sailed on to a beach for picnicking and big enough for whiffling for mackerel. She had to carry a Seagull model 40 under the after deck with a spare can of petrol, picnic baskets and so on. She must be light enough for dad and mum to get on and off a trailer. A robust 14 footer seemed to be about right.

I was tempted to ask Jack Holt to design this multi-purpose boat, but hesitated to put all Yachting World's baskets into one egg as it were.

I discussed my ideas with the late Charles E. Nicholson, a life-long friend and one of the world's greatest yacht designers. He had designed and built at his yard at Gosport, a small sailing boat for his grandchildren. He thought he could produce what I wanted. It was a wonderful

opportunity. So it seemed. But Nicholson's conception was far from what I had in mind. She was a lovely little boat, but no amateur could ever build her.

So I turned to another old friend, the late J. Laurent (Jack) Giles, famous for ocean races and a wide variety of successful craft. His boat, too, was a disappointment. She could be amateur built but that was about the only requirement she fulfiled.

Then O'Brien Kennedy, a young designer who had shown great originality with both racing dinghies and larger yachts, had a go. In fact, he drew two lovely designs but, somehow, neither completely filled the bill.

So, Jack Holt it was. When I gave him my lengthy list of requirements he seemed unperturbed and not the least put out. He thought he would have to make the mast easy to manage, and having made a few more sensible suggestions, departed to Putney. Within two days he was back with a set of plans. "Not enough freeboard", I said, "She has not only to be seaworthy and safe, she has got to look seaworthy and safe, otherwise you won't get mum near the boat let alone sailing in her".Even near the end of his life Jack still felt that the GP had too much freeboard. No argument could change my mind, so off he went accompanied by Beecher Moore who, being American, accepted the dictum that "The Customer is Always Right". A week later Jack telephoned to ask whether or not I was sailing anywhere in particular in Ellen Sophia, my small Nicholson cruiser, that weekend. I wasn't, so he said that, if convenient, he would meet me at Hamble, my home port and rang off. When I arrived that Friday afternoon, there was Jack, standing beside — guess what? — The GP14 prototype, rigged ready to launch. As I inspected her, there was every detail just as I had wanted it. She was faultless and I was speechless. After a long spell of silence, Jack could bear it no longer. "Aren't you going to say anything, skipper?" he asked anxiously. "Jack", I replied, "I think she is perfect".

So, we launched her, made her fast astern of Ellen Sophia and towed her away to Newtown Creek for a weekend of trials. We found no fault in her. Today she is fundamentally the same boat — in deference to mum, we gave her a smallish jib and no spinnaker — cost was of course, a consideration.

Dusty Pollock, who already had an enviable reputation for "Cadet kits", undertook to produce the "Build-her-Yourself" set of parts. He sailed at Aberdovey and the Aberdovey S.C. was the first club to adopt the GP as a club boat. As no one had thought of an insignia, we adopted the Bell (Bells of Aberdovey) nothing to do with Bell Woodworking & Co., which caused some confusion. Nevertheless, all Yachting World "Build-her-Yourself" boats owe a great debt of gratitude to the late Dusty Pollock, the owner of the Bell Woodworking Company. He was as good a joiner as Jack was a designer of small hard chine boats. He was also a loyal friend. He acted as Class Secretary from 1953—1954.

Jack is the only man in the world, to my certain knowledge, who can design a hard chine boat that does not look like a box and can hold its own with any similar round bilge boat.

The GP Fourteen Class was fortunate in that in the early days E. Howard-Davies was at the helm. He once asked me whether I thought it would be advisable to apply to become a R.Y.A. National Class. I advised him, in view of his own ability and that of his strong Committee, to go it alone because the R.Y.A. only thought about racing and would never understand the unique purpose of the GP Class. Today it is amongst the world's best known and best organised Classes.

by Group Captain E. F. Haylock
This article is taken from that written for the 25th. Anniversary Handbook, Ed.

Jack Holt
(1912 - 1995)

Jack Holt & Beecher Moore at 'Sailboat'

Jack Holt did more than any other individual to popularise dinghy sailing. He produced around 40 different dinghy designs during his lifetime. Nearly 130,000 boats were registered but double that number have probably been built.

He was responsible for the first Merlin design, while the Cadet, GP Fourteen and Enterprise gave thousands their first experience of sailing through Jack's budget-level, home built designs.

He learnt to sail with his brother on the tidal waters of the Thames in the 20's. Apprenticed to a cabinet maker, he gained the skills which enabled him to take over the boat repair business of his uncle. So started his career that was to make him the most famous and prolific dinghy designer and builder of all time.

He had immediate success with a design of an Int. Fourteen for river conditions and orders followed. Needing larger premises, he went into partnership with Percy Chandler, later Secretary of the 505 Class.

Something of a specialist in designing for the river, in 1936 his attention turned to the National 12. The war was only an interruption and he resumed building 12's in 1945. His belief that there was a need for a more economical boat than the Int.14, resulted in the 'Merlin' design, to be launched by Yachting World magazine. This soon outnumbered the 14's.

Around this time Beecher Moore joined Jack as his business partner and the two sailed together with considerable success in a number of 'Merlins'

In 1947 the 'Cadet' was launched, again through Yachting World, as an economical, entry-level racing dinghy for youngsters. It proved an immediate success and has prospered ever since.

The GP Fourteen followed in 1949, going into production the following year. Promoted actively by Yachting World Magazine it was an instant success worldwide, soon over 500 boats being built annually.

Jack followed this successful design with two more which were to add more glory to his reputation. The Enterprise and the Mirror Dinghy. The latter using the revolutionary 'stitch and glue' method of construction.

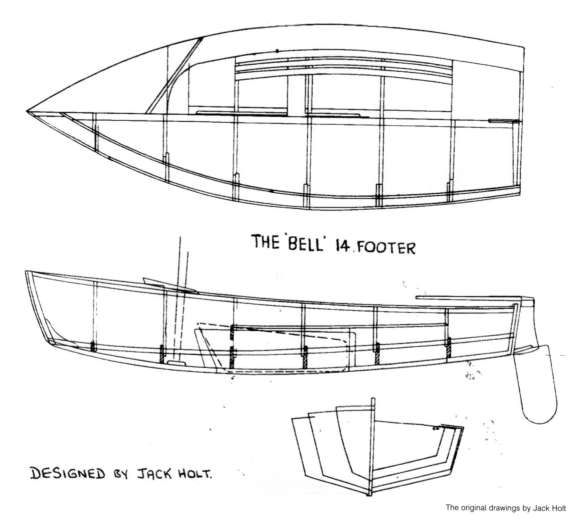

THE 'BELL' 14.FOOTER

DESIGNED BY JACK HOLT.

The original drawings by Jack Holt

In the late 50's he added boat fittings, spars and clothing to the business.

In 1973, retired to West Wittering, he pottered about the creeks of Chichester Harbour in his designs. In 1979 he was awarded the OBE for his services to sailing. Jack maintained his interests in his designs and became involved with the latest FRP version of the GP14.

Jack, a gentle and unassuming character, was always a welcome visitor at our Championships. Often unannounced and never seeking the limelight, he was secretly proud that he had been able to bring the joys of sailing to so many.

We are proud that, together with the other Classes he had helped to found, we could honour both Jack and Beecher Moore for their partnership of 50 years service to dinghy sailing at Sailboat in 1995.

Acknowledgements and thanks to Peter Cook and Yachts & Yachting for the basis of this article.

The GP14 and the men of Leicester

Searson Thompson

We who have had much to do with the GP have come to love the boat. I suppose that some of you are as sentimental as I and have only had one. Mine is 1490, built by myself in 1956 and, as recently as last year, managed, by pure fluke of course, to finish 2nd in a club trophy event.

I started sailing, most fortunately, at Aberdovey. It was in 1953, only a short time after the Class was formed. Those of you who know the beach there will remember that the sand is very soft and it requires a 'team' to retrieve a GP and bring it to the dinghy park. Some might say "Yes and a team of horses too". Well, being on holiday and instantly infatuated by these wonderful sailing boats, I knew of no others at the time. The only way I could get my hands on one of the GP's was to help pull it up the beach. It seems that GP75 got quite a lot of attention and the following year the same happened and her owner, recognising me, asked me out for a sail one evening. I had no idea at the time as to who he was. Incidentally, GP 75 was the first to be built at home from a kit by Searson Thompson, who was to become managing director of Bell Woodworking.

Well what is the purpose of this story, my thoughts and recollections of an aspect of the development of the GP? I have been involved with engineering design and development all my life. It is something I loved doing. Building the GP from scratch was just an extension of this. I was probably thinking of how to make hundreds instead of just one. At the same time to consider how and why it was what it was, where things went and why it was that shape.

Group Captain Haylock writing about the GP14, tells of his 'Build her yourself concept', and his list of requirements for a boat which ended up with dinghy designer, Jack Holt. Well, nine days from concept to launching the GP meant to me that there had to be a lot of poetic licence, or whatever one calls that sort of thing. There had been a story of old, told by several who are no longer with us, that the first prototype had ended up as a beehive. This supports the fact that Bell Woodworking in Leicester built the prototype. But was the boat launched at Aberdovey the first? Did Jack have the first one built near his workshops in London? Did the first/second boats exactly follow Jack's drawings? We have a copy of the first concept drawing shown to Group Capt. Haylock. A lot of work was done before the GP as we know it as a production boat, was built.

The first production YWGP14's (Yachting World GP14) were made in Leicester by Bell Woodworking and so was the prototype(s). Group Capt. Haylock and Dusty Pollock had been friends for some time so it was natural that these were built under the guidance of Dusty who had already the experience of producing the Cadet dinghy. The idea of producing a kit for these boats came from his wartime experience when his company manufactured beehives and possibly other items for the the war effort in a prefabricated form. We would call them kits or perhaps 'flatpack' today. His contribution to the war effort was considerable and unsung. But there was another side to Dusty. He was very much aware that the war had changed people, and their expectations. This fitted in with the views of Haylock. He set out to market a product which 'the man in the street' could build or buy at an affordable price. This gave him and her an opportunity to enjoy a sport hitherto confined to the few. It heralded the growth of sailing clubs on lakes and reservoirs throughout the country.

It would indeed have been a nine days wonder if it were only that long from concept to launch. I think not only of Dusty Pollock but also of the craftsmen at Bells', the number of times they had to stop and say "This just won't go, shall we do so and so?" A look at the forefoot on the concept plans tells its own story don't you think? And did any designer ever show the client his product without a tryout first? Where was that first launch? A secret location in the Midlands? I wonder, were you there?

So where do we go with these thoughts? I think we should quietly say a little thank you to those at Leicester who with Jack Holt, (for he must have been close by), developed Jack's concept of the GP. They made it possible for the boat to be produced economically and in large numbers: In both factory and in kit form, in garages everywhere. Above all it is a boat which has become one of the most loved and used sailing dinghies in the world.

Dusty chose to sail a GP, No.7 and was Secretary of the Association in 1952-53. 50 years on, it is still one of the most popular.

1	E. Howard Davies	Tan-y-Coed, Llanfair - P.G., Anglesey.	Kittiwake II	Dovey S.C.
2	D.H.Tildesley	237 Tetenhall Road, Wolverhampton.	Pimpernel	Dovey S.C.
3	O.E.Brookes	33a Stonehouse Road, Sutton Coldfield.	Quiver	Dovey S.C.
4	Col.F.R.Hulton	3 Penhelig Terrace, Aberdovey.		Dovey S.C.
5	D.M.Barlow	Redlands, Pedmore, Stourbridge,	Puffin	Dovey S.C.
6	T.Jarvis	17 Monmouth Drive, Sutton Coldfield.		Dovey S.C.
7	D.W.Pollock	The Cottage, Countesthorpe, Leicester.		Dovey S.C.
8	Maj.D.J.Underhill	Tregonwell, Aberdovey.	Red Shank	Dovey S.C.
9	F.H.Austen	12 Pembroke Avenue, Westbrook, Margate.	Four Winds	Broadstairs
10	G.F.Williams	The Slip, Buildwas, Nr. Ironbridge.	Madam X	Shropshire S
11	Miss M.E.Jervis & ors.	Murrayfield, Belle View Gardens, Shrewsbury.	Shearwater	Shropshire S
12	T.Carson Abbott	Hadley Park Farm, Wellington Shropshire.	Scarlett	Shropshire S
13	J. & A.Gough	Brooklyn, Christine Avenue, Wellington.	Jess	Shropshire S
14	N.Calvert Wilson	2 Woodlands Park, Shrewsbury.	White Wisp	Shropshire S
15	A.B.Taylor	Wenffrwd, Llangollen.	Gypsy	Shropshire S
17	Dovey S.C.	c/o J.B.Tyler, 43 Delves Crescent, Walsall.	Dorey	Dovey S.C.
18	D.R.Vale	68 Beacon Hill, Aldridge.	Curly	Dovey S.C.
19	P.J.Ward	72 Reddings Road, Moseley, Birmingham 13	Mizpah	Dovey S.C.
21	C.Lyth Hudson	The Roft, Oakfield Road, Shrewsbury.	Pegasus	Shropshire S
23	R.Birkett Evans	Bryn Dwr, Gresford, Near Wrexham.	Hawk	Shropshire S
24	Dr.L.D.Philp	Rivershill, St.Georges Crescent, Stanwix, Carlisle.	Jolly Roger	Bassenthwaite
25	J.W.Cane &·anr.	114 Totley Brook Road, Totley Rise, Sheffield.	Kestrel	Dovey S.C.
26	O.K.Dawes	46 Beaumont Road, Petts Wood, Kent.		Medway Y.C.
27	R.H.Crompton	Lily Cottage, Windermere.	Pintail	R.Windermere
28	D.H.Watson	Beech Lodge, Bowness-On-Windermere.	Aeolian	R.Windermere
29	R.Oddy	Bouverie Mount, Sunnyside, Kendal.	Stymie	R.Windermere
30	L.R.Witheridge	Kremal, Boscobel Road, Walsall.	Minx	Dovey S.C.
31	C.H.D.Acland + ors.	Box Trees, Crook, Kendal.	Pointer	R.Windermere
33	J.J.Campbell	765 Ormskirk Road, Pemberton, Wigan.	Joy	
34	J.Dunn	18 Crow Lane West, Newton-le-Willows.	Spray	Holyhead S.C
36	H.Waterhouse	The Mill House, 165 Moor Lane, Great Crosby.	Crinette	Blundellsand
38	T.A.Tomkins	19 Pages Lane, Great Barr, Birmingham 22a.	Gazelle	Dovey S.C.
39	S.R.Harfoot	32 Somerset Road West, Barry, Glam.	May	Penarth M.B.
40	J.D.Clay	16 Vernon Avenue, Linby, Notts.	Flamingo	
41	J.L.Ashford	Highfield, Hillwood Common Road, Sutton Coldfield.	Annina	New Quay S.C
42	R.E.Russell	16 Wharfdale Street, Wednesbury, Staffs.	Dipper	Dovey S.C.
45	R.E.Owen	3 Tan-y-Bryn Road, Holyhead.	Gem	Holyhead S.C
46	H.Farnell	154 Manor Way, Whitchurch, Cardiff.	Gareen Jr.	Penarth M.B.
47	Dr.J.V.Manning	Hill Cliff, Mill Lane, Rainhill.	Caltha	West Kirby S
48	S.Leggett R.H.WHITAKER	3 The Oaklands, West Kirby PRIORY HO., PRIORY RD. W.KIRBY	Tinkabel	West Kirby S
49	H.G.Mitchell	56 Ambrose Road, Cardiff.	Wingo	Penarth M.B.
50	Dr.T.Evans Jones	Balmain, Aberayron, Cards.	Gwylan	New Quay Y.C
51	S.Wyllie	69 Heath Park Avenue, Cardiff.	Giselle	

The first GP Listing

Aberdovey and
the Birth of the GP14

Aberdovey 1951

This article endeavours to portray the part that the Aberdovey Yacht Club played in the early development of this renowned dinghy. The historical facts were supplied by Searson Thompson, a keen sailor and a long serving member of the Dovey Yacht Club, and who was involved over many years, as Managing Director of The Bell Woodworking Company. A company responsible for producing the GP14 boats, both finished and in kit form.

In the post-war years, sailing was an activity that appealed to many, but proved too expensive and certainly beyond the reach of the working man. Designers of small boats like Uffa Fox, Jack Holt, Wyche & Coppack often used the traditional clinker built methods in their mainly 'one off' designs, but like the top class offshore racing fraternity, the Sopwith's and Lipton's, their craft were too exclusive and thereby expensive.

Group Captain Haylock, Editor of Yachting World, and Jack Holt, shared similar sailing interests, and both saw the need for a cheap easily produced boat, and so the 'car top' dinghy was evolved. The Cadet was one such, but still a 'one off' design.

The war had seen a rapid development of resin bonded marine plywood and adhesives used to produce torpedo boats, bridging pontoons and aircraft like the Mosquito and Magister. These

Searson Thompson - Aberdovey 1954

materials were readily available and proven to be well suited to mass production. So, gradually, the concept of a cheaply produced sailing dinghy began to emerge. At this point another 'player' arrived on the scene, Dusty Pollock, a woodworker and keen bee-keeper, who also sailed and was presently engaged in producing beehives in kit form in his factory.

All three, Jack Holt, Capt. Haylock and Dusty Pollack got together to exchange views and ideas. Dusty suggested expanding his experience of producing beehives in kit form to boat kits. They all agreed to proceed on these lines. This led to the eventual expansion of Pollack's business to form the Bell Woodworking Company Ltd.

It was a historic step and changed the face of dinghy building. It was possibly the first manufacturer to produce sailing dinghies in kit form to be assembled by amateurs. The kits were exported world wide.

The Yachting World Magazine decided to promote a 14ft. family dinghy, that could be sailed, rowed and motored. Jack Holt was asked to design such a boat. The plans had to be modified subsequently to suit the manufacturing processes to enable it to be produced in kit form. Eventually a prototype was built and taken down to Hayling Island, where all

GP14s Nos. 2, 6, 19 & 49 - Aberdovey YC Regatta July 2000

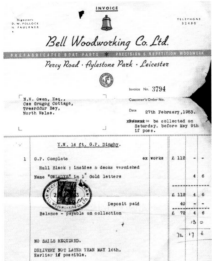

GP14 270 Original Receipt - 1953

the key people involved in its conception and manufacture, witnessed a highly successful trial. The question then arose, what shall we call it? The Yachting World Magazine said it was a General Purpose Dinghy and so it became known as the GP14.

At this time in 1949, the Dovey Yacht Club was looking for a general one-class dinghy to adopt. With the support of Howard-Davies and Brigadier Palmer, two keen members, the Bell Woodworking Co. was invited to bring down one of their new mass produced plywood dinghies for a trial. Despite some local scepticism it was put through its paces for several weeks on the River Dovey before being finally accepted. One snag remained, what type of insignia would be shown on the sail? The manufacturer already had a Bell logo displayed. This dilemma was finally resolved at a later date. Meanwhile the first ten dinghies were ordered with No.1 going to Howard-Davies and No.2 to Brigadier Palmer.

Several other clubs in Shropshire, Newquay, Holyhead and Windermere also adopted this new hard-chined, mass-produced plywood dinghy.

In 1951 its popularity prompted the formation of a Class Association, and at the inaugural meeting held in Whitmere, Shropshire, after a stormy session, when the issue of whether to call it a 'Bell' Class or a 'GP14', it was decided to call it the latter and the sail logo to be a representation of one of the mythical 'Bells of Aberdovey'.

The first GP14 race meeting was then held here in Aberdovey. You could be tempted to say that the 'Mother Club' had given birth to a lusty baby!

The first GP14 to be built from a Bell Kit by an 'amateur' was sailed extensively on the River Dovey. Its sail number was 75 (the numbering of sails was not controlled until later, when the Association took on the responsibility). Incidentally, early GP's, sail numbers 2, 6, & 64 are still active on the estuary here in 1997 !

It would be fitting to conclude that for the many, the chance to sail and race in an affordable dinghy, owes much to the pioneers who had the foresight and industry to carry out their vision.

Ed. Thanks go to the Dovey YC for this article published by them in 1997.

Memories of the early days of the GP14 Class
the Holyhead Sailing Club
and Two National Champions

Whitemere 1955. GP1 Howard-Davies (Aberdovey). GP 710 Peter Waine (Shropshire Sailing Club)

Trying to recall those very early days of the founding of the GP14 Class at the age of 82 years is proving very difficult. However, I shall try my best with the assistance of Gladys and friends. I sincerely hope that what little I can remember will help in compiling the history of the GP14 Class.

When I was a young lad in the 1930's I would go down to the harbour to watch the movement of craft on its waters, for as stated and also marked on the Admiralty Charts, Holyhead Harbour was a harbour of refuge for the old sailing ships. This part is now known as the promenade. I remember along its full length, every 100ft or so, a line of cast iron bollards to which the sailing ships, having first dropped anchor would lie, stern first, secured to the bollards. However, even so I have pictures and reports of craft from 15ft. to 30ft. competing in races round the harbour but as a young lad I was more interested in the miscellaneous craft with their clinker built hulls and cotton sails. The craft I was most interested in was the 14ft. Kingstown Wag which had a fleet of 10 or so competitors with a crew of three or four depending on the strength of the wind. When I left school and started as an apprentice boatbuilder in the marine yard at Holyhead in 1934 I built one such craft naming her 'SARAH' after my mother. This class of boat is no longer in Holyhead but is a big and popular class in Ireland.

Like all sailing clubs in this country, when war was declared in 1939 all sailing ceased. I was, before war was declared, in the Merchant Navy, and stayed there until 1946. On returning home and living with my parents I was very surprised to find that my friends had no interest in resuming racing in the harbour, so even though it took some time to create interest in forming a new club and getting craft on the water, it was not until 1951, following a race in my Kingstown Wag 'SARAH', that on coming ashore I was introduced to Mr Jim Dunn of Newton-le-Willows who spent every summer caravanning in Perth Dafarch, three miles out of Holyhead. He had just purchased from Bell Woodworking Co. Leicester, a GP14. He admitted that he had no idea how to sail it but would welcome advice etc. on how to do so. This was not the first GP I had seen, for when serving at the Outward Bound School at Aberdovey, I met Mr Howard-Davies who was also at the school teaching navigation etc. and also with his wife Gwen, running a hotel on the seafront. It was there that I saw the first prototype GP14 brought down to Aberdovey by Mr.D.Pollock of Bell Woodworking. Howard and I sailed her up and down the Dovey Estuary, with and against a very strong tide, much to the surprise of the locals on how well it performed.

To go back to my meeting with Mr.Dunn with his GP14 No.34 named 'SPRAY', was the turning point for its adoption by the Holyhead SC and in not too many years we had a fleet of 30 in very competitive racing.

Members of our club were not the type that would take their boats very far from home waters; the furthest they would venture was Traeth Bychan of The Red Wharf Bay SC and the Menai Straits for their GP14 Open Meetings. However, this changed when our sons, David and Edward, started sailing GP's. But more of that later.

To go back to the early days of the Class, I was inspired by Howard-Davies to attend meetings as the representative of the Holyhead SC and

THE G.P FOURTEEN NATIONAL CHAMPIONSHIP 1957
BASSENTHWAITE LAKE, 6th and 7th JULY

RESULTS

Searson Thompson, Aberdovey 1954

for N.Wales clubs, thus one of the first meetings I recall was in the winter of 1952 in Shrewsbury when very heavy snow had fallen the night before our departure and Howard, being a fast driver, we were sliding all over the road and lucky at bends that no other cars were coming towards us. Meetings these days comprised at best of six members.

I cannot remember all of them but the minute book should reveal all including the first Open Meetings and National Championships. When possible, I would attend Open Meetings, the furthest away being the National Championship at Hamble and another at Bassenthwaite pictured on page 21. No doubt you may recall quite a number of members both living and those passed on. The photostat copy is when the Nationals were held in Holyhead in 1956 which shows our David being presented with a prize having crewed for Howard, the Championship being won by C.D.Grace of Penarth.

Going back to Bassenthwaite Nat. Championships in 1957 I had Edward crew for me for a couple of light wind races. In the second race following the second round of a triangular course, the wind came up very quickly and with strong gusts had me spilling wind, with the boom trailing in the water which frightened Edward and resulted in me retiring and putting Edward off sailing for two years. His main interest became cricket, but one day David was short of a crew and Edward agreed to crew for him which started him off in a successful racing career.

The rest you know because both were to become National Champions in the Class. Even though neither sail a GP14 now, their interest in the Class is as strong as ever. David is the Captain on Cruise liners and Edward an International World class yachtsman, proving that from the GP14 Class some world famous mariners have roots in the Class. Edward is currently coach to the Spanish entry to the Americas Cup.

Editor's note: Edward manages the successful TV series of ULTRA racing, the first regular TV programme to bring the excitement of our sport to the public. David is currently Captain of "Saga Rose" having for some time been Staff Captain of the QE2. Norman at 82, regularly races in various boats including his own 'Half Rater'.

Norman Warden-Owen

The GP14's
& The Royal Windermere Yacht Club

In the early summer of 1952, Mr.R.H.Crompton visited Bells at Leicester and ordered a GP14 No.27, 'Pintail' which he entered in an all-comers race in July of that year with C.H.D. Acland (Cubby) as his crew. Two months later Cubby was to take delivery of No. 31, 'Pointer', both dinghies being kept at White Cross Bay.

Editor's Note: Seven years later 1959, Cubby was to become our third President.

Impressed by the qualities and performance of the boat, and by the enthusiasm of their owners, W.B.Smith, who was then Commodore, offered club membership to a small band of new or potential boat owners who had been assiduously canvassed and cajoled into ownership by Messrs. Compton and Acland with the active support of P.F. Scott, a member of one of the old yacht club families and himself one of the keenest protagonists of the new class and the owner of No123, 'Bunting'. It was agreed that the new GP14 Class Association which had been formed, should be recognised by the club, and that the Windermere boats should race under the Class Rules, modified where necessary to meet local requirements. (Spinnakers for example were not allowed).

A racing programme with points scoring on a system used by the 17ft. Class was arranged and a racing fee of 10/- per year. Saturday afternoons, when the official starters were available and Thursday evenings, were the times most favoured by the new Class for dinghy racing. The GP's had arrived on Windermere.

At the end of its first racing season the Class was a dozen strong and perhaps it is worth recording the names of the original boats and their owners. In the early days numbers were allocated in blocks, Nos. 27-29 & 31 being in the first batch, 122 to 130 the second.

Editor's Note: It is noteworthy that Nos.23, 26, 27, 122 & 125 are still appearing in our member boat list in this millennium year 2000.

At first, the GP's raced together and on even terms with the Firefly's and rivalry was keen. Patronising references to 'picnic boats' were countered by charges of discomfort and downright cruelty to Firefly crews exposed always to the imminent danger of decapitation. Although not specially designed for racing, the GP's proved their capabilities, especially in a strong breeze, and in winning the C.J.E.Hall Challenge Cup presented to the winner of a series of races, 'Pointer' (C.J.D. & O. Acland) earned the distinction of being the only GP to appear on a Firefly Challenge Cup. Forty six dinghy races were arranged that year, five or six to a Series, and the first invitation team race in which the GP's took part were sailed on Saturday, September 14th, when ten teams, four from the club and six visiting teams, competed. The final was fought out between Sheffield Viking and The Royal Windermere YC. Windermere winning by two points, this being the difference between a fourth and fifth place stubbornly made by John Dewhurst a young Firefly helmsman who, after a false start, subsequently fell overboard. Refusing to be deterred by these misfortunes

he clambered aboard again and sailed into fourth place by one second, so enabling the club to win its own first invitation event.

'Pointer' finished the season as leading boat with 'Pintail' and 'Pab' in second and third places, and went on to win the first GP14 National Championship which was sailed in October at Whitemere under the Burgee of the Shropshire SC.

It was not long before the influx of new members created an unexpected problem whose solution became increasingly difficult as the dinghy class prospered, the problem of providing space, not only for member's cars, but for their dinghies. Extra land having been leased from the adjoining Old Fallbarrow Estate, a working party directed and enthusiastically led by the Commodore (W.B.Smith), set to work one September Sunday in 1952. Strange cries of "Timber" echoed across the hard, as an odd company of amateur lumberjacks (and lumberjills), hacked, cleared and burned the 'jungle' and levelled the ground to make car and dinghy park extensions. This was the first of a number of working parties which in the years that followed, converted extensions of the club's territory into parking space in 1960 for approximately 80 dinghies.

In spite of the keen rivalry and competition between them during the first summer, the question of the relative speeds of Firefly's and GP14's was still unresolved when the season ended. It was decided therefore that they should continue to race together, but should compete for separate prizes and because of the considerable disparity of skill and experience which existed between dinghy helmsmen, a number of handicap races should be interspersed in the Series races. The first series of handicap races appeared on the fixture card for 1953. Individual handicaps, increased by each flag won by the boat, were assessed on the results of the previous races and were posted in the club before each handicap event. The system was never very popular or successful and two years later the Dinghy Committee decided to drop the handicap races and substitute a number of races for novices, to encourage those helmsmen who had never won a dinghy race organised by the club, other than a handicap race.

Regulations to ensure the observance of safety conditions were approved (GP's had to carry 600lbs. buoyancy and two life jackets). Parking spaces were allotted in the dinghy park according to the number of starts made during the previous year. The racing fee was increased in stages to 30/- in 1958, plus a contribution of 5/- to the prize fund, out of which, from time to time, additional challenge cups and trophies were bought. Single handed races were introduced in 1955 and it was ruled in 1957 that, except in these events, dinghies must carry a crew as well as a helmsman when racing. About this time too a number of the courses were duplicated so that they could be sailed either way round according to the course chosen for the 17ft. Class. The need for this provision was vividly brought home one Saturday afternoon when in a moderately fresh breeze the yacht and dinghy fleets converged on Hen Holme turning mark which they rounded in opposite directions. There were thrills in plenty and many anxious moments, though fortunately collisions were avoided on that occasion, it was thought imprudent to tempt fate a second time.

An idea by D.A.White led to another innovation - the Open Marathon races for Firefly's and GP's. Arranged near the end of the programme when the stress and strain of striving for 'points' and 'average' honours were over, the marathon was just the right climax to the season's sailing and social activities. The first race in a good north wind had two gruelling beats up to Wray and finished at White Cross Bay for lunch; the second covered a course between Low Wood, Wray and Pull Pyke, finishing at Waterhead for tea ; and the third was a run from Waterhead to Hen Holme with a beat back to F.B.A. before finishing on the Hen Holme line. It was a full day of good sailing and good fun to be remembered in the winter months ahead and was so successful and so enjoyed, that Marathon races became an annual event. In the GP Fleet, 'Pointer' won the series on that occasion; 'Flook' (M.A.Higham), took first place in 1958 and 'Ebb Tide' (E.Twiname, Bassenthwaite SC) in 1959.

The members of Bassenthwaite SC., this time were no strangers to Windermere. In November 1951, a few months after he had taken delivery of 'Pointer', C.H.D.Acland took the late I.M.Banner-Mendus, President of the GP Fourteen Association 1958-59, and others from the West Cumberland for a cruise, and so claims to have inspired the Bassenthwaite Sailing Club which adopted the GP Fourteen as its only class. From the beginning, relations between the two clubs were most friendly and in June 1953 the first of a series of team races took place between them, since when both home and away fixtures have been arranged every year.

The most noteworthy event in the history of the GP section in these early years however, was the Yachting World GP Fourteen Open Championship, which, on the invitation of the club, was sailed on Windermere under the club's burgee on Saturday and Sunday July 24th & 25th, 1954.

Norman & Philip Quarry

The problem of accommodating so many boats between races was partly solved by the provision of a floating boom moored in the bay, and catering arrangements for the large gathering of competitors, crews, supporters and visitors, were cheerfully undertaken by lady members.

While the gaily coloured hulls and sails of so many small craft made a wonderful picture on the lake, the massed start posed the Championship officials a difficult problem and there was much bumping and boring both on the line and round the marks. The course was set in the North Lake with a variable starting line to allow for changes in wind and conditions were almost ideal. Hope ran high that 'Pointer', which had won the first Championship in 1952 and been runner-up in 1953, would take advantage of sailing in home waters to bring the Bell Trophy back to Windermere, but it was not to be. 'Kittiwake II' (E.Howard-Davies, Dovey SC), was first in three of the four races and easily won the Series. 'Pab', (sailed by N.Bacon), was the first Windermere boat to finish and 'Pointer' came in seventh. The Windermere Trophy, a silver salver, was presented in 1954 by the club to the GP Fourteen Class for award annually to the winner of the second race. The Championship series was won for the first time by 'Ariel' (G.Mathison, Bassenthwaite SC). Also sailed on Windermere four years later, on June 21st. and 22nd. 1958.

And so in 1960 we come to the Club's Centenary year with forty four GP's on the Club register and over fifty club races, in addition to team and open events, arranged for them during the season; with club membership bursting at the seams, greatly improved club facilities and extensive car and dinghy parking arrangements, the GP's have settled in. They have found their sea legs and have established a good sound footing in the life of the club as well.

The GP was adopted by the club in the hope that the introduction of a new dinghy class might help to inject new life into its activities and revive its fortunes, which in the aftermath of the war had been flagging.

Perhaps the GP owners, in acknowledging the privileges and enjoyment which membership of the club has brought them, may be pardoned a little conceit that they on their part have brought something to the club. In fulfilling the purposes for which they were admitted they have justified their Class title in a way scarcely contemplated when it was first thought of. Picnic boats perhaps, but certainly General Purpose Dinghies!

Ed. Taken from an article published in the book celebrating the Centenary of the Royal Windermere Yacht Club in 1960.

Shropshire SC

The Shropshire Sailing Club has a unique place in the history of the GP14. Not only did it host the first National Championship, but from its members came several of the early committee which laid down such fine foundations for the future of the Association. Dr. Ryle hosted the first committee meeting at his home and for many years a committee meeting was held at the club on the occasion of the Open Meeting held in September.

The club, situated near to Ellesmere, is one of the most delightful locations in the country. It is not a large lake but sufficient to test the best of dinghy sailors. Though surrounded by trees, it could produce some violent spasms of wind which would send sails and feathers a flying.

Well known for their hospitality, the club held a most successful end of season Open Meeting which became a 'must' in the circuit. No GP club dared to 'double up' on their date.

Although a small club it has produced many members who have distinguished themselves on the Championship circuit.

The Clubs

One of the key features, in the early days, was the way in which the Class was quickly adopted in clubs. At least ten clubs were represented when a Committee was formed to represent the owners, Dovey, Shropshire, Holyhead, New Quay, Penarth, Royal Windermere, Royal Temple, Broadstairs, Hoylake, quickly followed by Bassenthwaite, West Kirby, South Yorkshire, Hamble River and Folland Aircraft. Other clubs soon followed as the sport rapidly developed during the 1950's. Names like Bolton, Chase, Frensham Pond, Solway, South Staffordshire and various clubs in the Plymouth area appear. Indeed, by 1952, there were around 50 clubs recognised as having a GP14 Fleet, some, like Combs, being exclusively for the Class.

Clubs began to run Open Meetings for the Class and, as the number of clubs increased, so the need for regional championships developed. These commenced in 1956 with a north and a south of England Championship and others in Wales and Northern Ireland. A Scottish Championship followed in 1957.

By 1958, the Association's list of events had 50 Opens, Regattas, Championships etc. recorded, all over the country from May to September. The fact that the National Championship in Plymouth clashed with the Northern Ireland Championship on the same weekend in July shows that the multiplicity of events brought problems early on! In the same year, some 90 clubs were recorded as having recognised fleets, while another 200 were known to have members sailing a GP14! Nevertheless, it is interesting to note the clubs that had the largest fleets, Bassenthwaite 45, Bolton 50, Chase 50, Frensham Pond 40, Nantwich & Border Counties 45, Northampton 54, South Staffordshire 40 and West Kirby 85! In general, clubs sailing on restricted - even small - waters seemed to succeed best for the Class. This is a factor that is still evident today. Perhaps that is because the

View from Chelmarsh SC Clubhouse

enthusiasm of a few individuals makes a bigger impact than in a large club on a large water, where a higher performance boat may come into its own.

The continued growth of the Class encouraged a significant change from 1963 with the initiation of 8 'Championship' areas, and a consequent effect on the structure of the Committee, with representation being based on those areas. Some, initially strong like South Wales, were strong because of the tradition of sailing in the area. Others, like the Midlands, North

Chelmarsh SC Clubhouse

West and London areas were going to be more important in the long term because of the sheer size of population within those Areas. The development of the motorway network, with its simpler lines of communication, has also had an impact on the Class and the sport in general.

Today, it can be seen that the original clubs are still there, with large fleets. To them have been added some others. Derwent Reservoir is an outstanding example of the effect of a single-minded person who caught anyone coming to the club to start sailing, diverting them into the GP14 camp! With some 70 boats recorded, it is the largest single club. However, with four clubs on its banks, the Welsh Harp Reservoir in London is believed to have more than 100 GP14s.

As Open Meetings developed, some areas wanted to find out who was the local champion of such events. The North West Area were first to have a Trophy and Series in 1968, supported by 12 clubs. The Midland Area soon followed, and most others in due course.

Clubs had also developed outside the British Isles. Many of these clubs arose from British forces being stationed around the Commonwealth. The first to be affiliated, in 1955, was at Penang SC, in Malaysia. The next year boats were being exported to the United States. That year also saw the Constitution amended to permit Branch Associations to be formed. By 1958, group members were established in Nigeria, Zimbabwe (then Southern Rhodesia), Canada and Malaysia. Branch Associations were formed in North America in 1959, South Africa, Australia and India in 1962. Ireland was reconstituted as a Branch Association in 1979 while an unlikely one had been created in Finland in 1978, where several people living at the lakeside town of Varkaus built their own boats.

In 1968, the Class had recorded fleets at more than 50 clubs around the world. Although contact has now been lost with many of these, it is apparent from various sources that many of the boats are still there. Some, like the 46 boats recorded at Ceylon Motor Yacht Club in Sri Lanka are rejoining the Association as active members. Meanwhile, the change in the political climate in South Africa has also refreshed the ties in the Class and led to revival of interest.

Today, the Class is accepted by the International Sailing Federation, the world governing body, as an International Class. It is seen as a 'classic' design worthy of recognition.

The People

"You join us for the boat, you stay with us for the people"

No review of the G P Fourteen dinghy could be complete without mention of some of the many people who have helped to make the Class. Some have been well-known sailors, champions or simple racers. Others have been helpful to the Class by their passive support. With an average 'life' in the GPs perhaps of three years, it is thought that not less than 300,000 people have regularly sailed the boat at one time!

Looking back at the list of early members, it is noticeable that there were many doctors! The nature of the GP14 Class must have had a special appeal. Of course, some of the names appear in other parts of this book. Howard Davies has to be in a special category, with Grp. Capt. Haylock, Jack Holt and Dusty Pollock. They all got the boat from the 'drawing board' and into the Clubs. Some of the early characters are (at the time of writing) still with us. Dr Roger Seal of New Quay, a pathologist, who was a member of the original Committee and well able to spin yarns of those days. He is reputed to have built a series of GP14s in a post-mortem room. Searson Thompson too, was part of the Bell Woodworking team that developed the kits and played a role on the Committee. Norman Warden Owen was another early Committee member and father of two past National Champions, David and Edward. Edward Warden Owen has, of course, gone on to become a master helmsman in offshore racing, while David has become Captain of a Cruise Liner.

'Les Femmes' with Eddie Ramsden at the 1989 National Championship, Mumbles YC

Some members were distinguished in other fields. Sir John Cockcroft appears in the list. He received a Nobel Prize for his work at Cambridge in nuclear physics. Others assisted the Class by their indirect involvement. Harold and Norma Cragg successfully ran Leigh Dinghy Stores for many years as a specialist dinghy chandler and then attended many Nationals; Robin Webb carried a similar role in the Midlands; while Frank Chapman's skills were in writing for the newspapers. Jimmy Fewster, a Northumberland farmer, and self-made millionaire, who had ridden on the Wall of Death before World War 2, sailed GPs at Greenlee and Royal Windermere, then went on to sponsor Solings for the Montreal Olympics. His chosen method was to buy and loan an International Soling to promising young helms; at one stage, he bought so many that he is reported to have caused a market shortage in Britain!

Richard Estaugh

Undoubtedly, it is those who won races that spring most readily to mind. The list of past National Champions holds many famous names. 'Cubby' Acland, from Windermere was the first - he was a gentleman sailor, who became President in due course. Next was Harold Norbury, then crewed by his son Cliff - subsequently known for many years work with Proctor Masts and the Royal Yachting Association. That same Cliff Norbury was Chairman of the Sailing Committee of the International Sailing Federation (ISAF) when the GP14 was granted international status in 1999/2000. Ian Willis was only seventeen when he won the Championship in 1961, by far the youngest winner of the Trophy. He won again in 1973 and 1978. Then there are two characters used to the sea in their occupation of fishing, Jack Pallot and Pete Currie who, in 1966 and 1969 respectively, won in the breeziest conditions. A select few appear elsewhere in this book. Quite a crop of champions went on to become famous as sailmakers. First among these is John McWilliam, a former RAF pilot from Northern Ireland, who in 1967 had "sailed a rather elderly boat as fast as any in the fleet and did not figure in the final reckoning by a series of misfortunes"! He won in 1968! Brian Hayes' win in 1972, with apprentice sailmaker Dick Batt as crew, led him into the sail business soon after. Much the same could be said of Ian Southworth who had been joint World Champion in 1983 and had the National title in 1988 and 1990. But then he went onto fame in bigger boats. That is even more true of one who never won a GP14 title, but certainly gained from experience learnt in the Class. Lawrie Smith had come through Club sailing in the North West with an ambition. He became America's Cup helm in 1983 and now regularly features in the Ultra series on television and major offshore races. Nor is he the only GP14 sailor to have sailed in the America's Cup, for John Wright (junior) from USA also holds that distinction, being the tactician on the winning Stars and Stripes at Freemantle. Edward Warden-Owen too was the helm of White Crusader for most of the same campaign. Another sailor to achieve top results in several Classes is Neil Marsden who won in 1984 and still participates. Yet another from the North West is Simon Relph, who figured strongly in the 1980s. If the number of wins counts as stature, Richard Estaugh with 11 National titles, starting in 1979, plus 5 World titles, would stand loftily above all others. A quiet and modest person

Honorary Life Members Mary Igglesden and George Mainwaring

who followed the others into sailmaking and has developed his own multi-faceted business, he has become a core figure in the Class. Another sailmaker who joined the Class about this time was Michael McNamara. He was winning crew for Mike Holmes in the 1980 National Championship and took several Area titles at this period. His advice, readily given, was of great value to the Class. These are very different personalities from the days of Bank Manager Alan 'Sally' Setford (a large and gregarious figure, who graced many later events with his presence), Burton Allen (the first Northern Ireland winner of the British Championship), Bill Morris (crewed by son, Peter - another large and jolly figure) and quiet young Martin Jolleys. One who had a sudden burst of fame was Andrew Read who, with crew Justine Felice, was, perhaps, an unexpected winner of the second World Championship at Thorpe Bay in 1971.

Championships are made up of many other personalities. The North West Area had more than its fair share for some years. (Sir) Eric Driver, Frank Cooper and John Barnes all vied for the top results in their Area, but never won the National title. All were imbued with the 'Corinthian' spirit and the Class benefitted from their participation. Harold Barnes, who learnt to sail with his father 'Big Jack' left the Class after winning the junior title, but went on to become a 5-0-5 World Champion. The Twiname name figures amongst the Class legends. Father, Alec, was a civil engineering contractor in Cumbria who sailed at Bassenthwaite Lake and earned a reputation for his wily cunning on the water, and an enviable reputation for eccentric behaviour at social functions! His son, Eric, was a superb helm too and went onto become an authority on Team racing and the Rules of racing before his tragic and all too early death. A charity established in his name enables the RYA annually to run a national inter-regional youth championship. Of course, there are many others who were successful at Area level and made an impact nationally but never quite made the 'gold' podium. In the late 1970s and early '80s, brothers Roger and John Mee put in many excellent results. In the same era, Alan Johnson and crew Dave Garlick came across from the Enterprise Class and never quite matched their performance in that domain.

If all of these were from one Area, it was not the only one producing front runners. The Welsh Harp in London gave the Class great sailors like David Bridgewater, Don Williamson, Dave Gilbert and John Reynolds. In Scotland, Graham McKerrigan proved himself eventually as a better Race Officer than winning helm. He has displayed great talent in that direction at Championship level.

Nick Brook, winner of NBCYC Open Meeting, receiving his prize from Dorothy Sandbach

Many others have contributed to the Class, by participation at all levels. John Salomonson (known widely as 'Solly') first won an Area Championship in 1972 in the South West. He held 3 Area titles in each of 1976 and 1977 and only the North East and South East titles have eluded him. His travelling around the country, which still continues, makes some sort of record in itself. Martin (Toby) Taylor is another Midlands sailor who is instantly recognised, not only for his motorbike stories, but also for many successes in his extensive travels. Past Secretary Roy McCaig travelled widely too and was 'Mr GP' to many, though he rejected the title as applicable only to Howard Davies (Ed. He was rather touched by the title!). George Mainwaring, John Tyler, Peter Sandbach and Bill Sherwen

Neil Thompson

are all names that would be linked to measuring and technical matters. David Smith, from Combs, operated the main Class 'grapevine' through the late1970s and early 1980s, both as Area Representative and later in charge of communications.

And then there have been famous crews. Tony Cole was crew for Richard Estaugh on many occasions. A first rate helm himself, he set the highest standards of ability and action. Peter Chester crewed for Howard Davies, as a merchant seaman cadet at HMS Conway and, although now a Merlin Rocket helm, still retains a close interest in the Class, having bought back his own favourite boat. Some have passed through the Class on the way to success. Cathy Foster's name is linked with Olympic campaigns in the 470 Class (where she sailed against all-comers to success) but, as her family were members at Frensham Pond, she learned her skills crewing for her father in a GP14.

Although designed as a boat for amateur construction, the Class has inevitably seen most boats built by professionals. There have been many such builders, principally for wooden boats, with a few gaining expertise in plastic construction. The strong character of some is clearly expressed in their boats. Pete Nickless gained a reputation as a supplier of fast boats when he took carefully selected bare hulls from Bell Woodworking and finished them in his own manner. John Balance (of Bossom's Boatyard in Oxford) was influential by his assistance with advice on improving the plastic hulls produced by Bourne Plastics. Alistair Duffin in Belfast has come from a family of quality joiners and ensures that his boats are readily recognised as special by individualistic touches. Barry Richards built up his Don Marine business with wooden boats too, but went on to develop plastic boats far beyond the original simple design that came from the first glassfibre hulls produced by Bourne Plastics.

If all these names are male, it must not be assumed that women were not notable throughout the history of the Class. One of the earliest to win races was Miss W P H Penman from Solway who won the Scottish Championship in 1959 and 1960. She came from a locally active sailing family. Peggy Robinson, a journalist with the Daily Express, joined the Committee in 1966 as North East Area Representative. Her task was to become

Media attention for World Champion Richard Estaugh during the Skerries SC 1997 Championship

the first Editor of the Class magazine. It started as a newsletter, titled 'Mainsheet', but quickly changed to 'Mainsail'. Through 15 issues over 5 years, she brought a punchy independent style that has rarely been matched. Meryl Gover brought the attention of the Committee to the need to satisfy the ideas of those who simply sailed for pleasure, and helped to develop cruising events. Muriel King had a simple mission. Despite being of an age where one should put one's feet up (now past 90 years!), she approached any that came to Derwent Reservoir SC and got them into a GP14. Her enthusiasm for sailing is truly infectious still and the Class has honoured her for her remarkable efforts in making the Club into the largest GP14 Club of all.

A few others deserve mention. When the RYA first recognised the need for a Committee to review and improve Race Management, they turned to Roy McCaig for his experience, but another was to have a lasting relationship too. George Wilson had sailed Wayfarers. He had been in the Navy during the war and had returned to Britain with Shell Oil for whom he had worked in Holland. He had a sharp mind and a keen interest both in race management and protests. He soon became a regular visitor to Championship events and was welcomed for his experience. As a Race Officer of International standing, Tony Lockett has had an influence also and the mantle of Race Management has fallen upon him. More recently, the Class has welcomed John Buckingham as Protest Chairman, though he too has never sailed a GP14.

There are many more names that have enriched the GP14 Class. One thing that they have all had in common is a sense of loyalty to the Class.

Ireland -
the hidden influence on GPs

When we came to write this chapter it rapidly became apparent that the GP enthusiasts in Ireland had contributed a great deal to many aspects of the social development of the Class and the technical evolution of the boat. To put matters in context, Ireland is an island of $5^{1}/_{2}$ million people, or about 7% of the combined population of Britain and Ireland. The number of Irish members of the Association represents 9% of the equivalent figure, and at around 200 members, in area terms Ireland ranks 4th after the Midlands and East Coast, North West, and London and South East Areas.

In the beginning ....

A few individuals had built GPs in the early 50s but it was not until 13th September 1955 that a group of GP people from around Belfast Lough held a meeting at Whitehead, the home of County Antrim Y.C., and formed the Northern Ireland Branch of the Yachting World General Purposes 14 foot Sailing

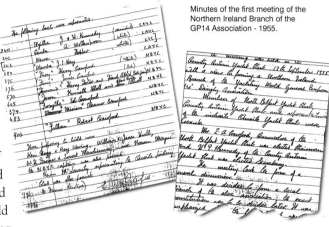

Minutes of the first meeting of the Northern Ireland Branch of the GP14 Association - 1955.

Dinghy Association. Clubs represented at the meeting, besides County Antrim Y.C., were North Belfast Y.C. and Quoile Y.C. from Strangford Lough.

Ernie Crawford, Commodore of North Belfast Y.C., was elected first Chairman with Hugh Kennedy of County Antrim as Honorary Secretary. At this time there were about a dozen GP14s in the area, and one of the main topics discussed was the differences between the home built boats.

During the autumn of 1955 members of Quoile Y.C. decided to adopt the GP, and construction started on six boats, numbered 881 to 886. Some idea of the egalitarian aspects of the Class can be seen from the backgrounds of the owners, namely, a council workman, a gardener, a dentist, an electrician, a civil engineer and a newsagent. Many of these boats turned out to be from 150 to 300 lbs overweight and in subsequent years some pretty drastic weight reduction modifications had to be undertaken.

A further meeting was held at Holywood Y.C. on 21st January 1956 where the guest speaker was Jack Austin, the Honourary Secretary of the GP Fourteen Class Association in Britain. Twelve owners were represented including Hugh Kennedy, whose GP 240, 'Elgitha', was the earliest number in Ireland, Ernie Crawford, whose family owned three GPs, Kevin

Ernie Mawhinney - doyen of the Irish GP Fleet - pictured sailing 'Ventura' with his son David

McLaverty from Quoile, and Ernie Mawhinney who indicated his intention to build a boat called 'Ventura', GP 796, which he sails competitively to this day, making him the doyen of the Class in Ireland.

Ken Dunlop proposed that County Antrim Y.C. be hosts for the inaugural Northern Ireland Championship and an entry fee of 5 shillings (25p) was agreed. Some years later Ken's career was to take him to Scotland where he continued his involvement with the GP Association, becoming President in 1965 and later a Trustee.

The first A.G.M. of the Northern Ireland Branch was held at Holywood Y.C. on 28th October 1956 when it was agreed that Larne Y.C. should be the venue for the 1957 Championship, a decision which had to be rescinded due to transport difficulties and petrol rationing! An interesting note from the following year's A.G.M. was that a majority of members were against wearing lifejackets.

1959 saw Larne's John McWilliam, later to found McWilliam Sailmakers, and Burton Allen from Ballyholme Y.C. join the committee and Ken Dunlop take over as Chairman. Unhappily in 1959 there was recorded the first fatal drowning accident involving a GP in Strangford Lough.

The 1959 Championship was held in Larne Lough and there is a tale told about one of the races where a sudden severe gust capsized a number of boats. Rescue cover in those days was usually provided by local boatmen and one such, a man of few words from a well known boat building family, had the capsize chaos pointed out in the following terms:

"Look Ned, the Reverend Gordon is in the water - we must go and save him! "Never worry" says Ned, wryly as he picked his way through the chaos of upturned boats "Gordon has been saved already".

In 1960 Jeckells Sails loaned two suits of the newly fangled terylene sails to the Northern Ireland Branch. Paul Rowan from Larne joined the Committee, and Burton Allen of Ballyholme Y.C. was elected Honorary Secretary in 1961, and that club set about building six boats to help grow the Class. It was he who took a strong stand on the wearing of lifejackets, or buoyancy aids as they have become known. His influence led to them being introduced as mandatory in the Class sailing instructions.

In the following year Graham Chambers from Quoile Y.C. took over as Chairman. Some, later to become famous GP names, Bill Whisker from Ballyholme, Doctors Curly Morris and Michael Hill from East Antrim B.C. in Larne, joined the Committee.

Enthusiasm for the GP was now at a high pitch and around 1963/64 saw the Class being adopted by clubs south and west of Belfast, like Rush S.C., Kilbarrack S.C in Dublin Bay, Mullingar right in the middle of the country and Lough Erne Y.C. and Sligo Y.C. in the west. There were approximately 140 boats in the country by 1963 and support for the Northern Ireland Championship had reached around 28 boats. Regattas were also a very popular meeting place for GPs and the Regatta Series in Belfast Lough, and the Regatta Week in Strangford Lough in July, particularly, operated like a mini Championship.

In the mid-60s there was a move to travel to the British Championship which was perceived to be the premier event in terms of numbers and competition, and the Irish sailors wanted to test themselves against the best. Later in this chapter we detail some of the many stories about going to events outside Ireland and the ensuing successes, but suffice to say the urge to look outwards helped introduce Irish GPs to new and wider horizons which, in retrospect, was good for them, and equally good for other parts of the GP world.

Team photograph - Llandudno 1967

Bill Sleat from Ballyholme Y.C. was elected Honorary Secretary in 1966 followed by fellow club member Peter Duffy in 1968. The importance of Ballyholme as a GP club became more evident as its GP fleet grew to 33 boats in 1968, and the strength in depth of its members' racing capabilities, led by Bill Whisker and Burton Allen, made it a dominant influence on the Class. This pre-eminence led to the club being invited to host the British Championship in 1969, the only time it has been sailed outside England, Wales and Scotland. It was generally considered to have been a very successful event with 109 entries, and it offered the prospect of Ballyholme going on to a four year cycle as host for the Championship.

Widening the reach of the Association

Around the middle 60s there was a realisation that the Class had developed south and west in Ireland, with 127 boats in the north and 67 in the south. This necessitated a change in the name and regional organisation of the Class which was to help drive the Class forward. The initial name of the Association was changed to 'The GP14 Class Association of Ireland'.

1970 saw Ireland being sub-divided into four areas, A,B,C and D for the purposes of election of Area Representatives, and from that point on the membership of the Committee became representative of the growth of the Class in the greater Dublin area and the east coast, and later, further south to Cork Harbour. In 1972 the areas were re-drawn based on the natural boundaries of the four provinces and thereafter the Class was organised around Ulster in the north, Leinster in the east, Munster in the south and the vast area of the west known as Connaught.

In 1972 one of the driving forces of the Class in Sligo Y.C., Gus Henry, succeeded Graham Chambers as Chairman of the Association, and in 1971, another major influence on the future of the Class, Pat Murphy from Kilbarrack S.C. in Dublin Bay, took over as Honorary Secretary from Paul Rowan. Pat had first come into contact with GPs when he had been in Whitehead, and later in Dundalk S.C., and he was active in setting up the Munster area when he travelled to a meeting in Cork on 3rd November 1973, at which John Cotter from Cove S.C. became the first representative.

Throughout its life the GP Association in Ireland has adopted a somewhat independent stance, and has been able to work its way around all the social and political changes which have influenced its member's everyday activities. Aside of those complex issues, it has had to contend with two national sailing bodies, the R.Y.A.'s Northern Ireland Branch and the Irish Yachting Association, later to become the Irish Sailing Association.

From its earliest days the I.Y.A. insisted on personal membership for anyone competing in Championships organised by clubs within its jurisdiction. In contrast, the R.Y.A. required that anyone who was a member of a club affiliated to it qualified to compete in Championships. This caused confusion at the 1975 Irish Championship in Fenit S.C. in Tralee Bay where the Race Officer maintained all competitors should be members of the I.Y.A., Generally, however, the Class turned a blind eye to requirements of this nature as they were too impracticable to implement.

In 1974, after an idea by Tom Jobling, the Class introduced a Travellers' Trophy which set out to encourage groups of GP sailors to support Championships and Open Events.

The heyday of the Class

By the mid to late 70s dinghy sailing in general, and GPs in particular, had reached its heyday. Class records show that by 1979 there were 16 clubs in Ulster with GP fleets totalling 170 boats; in Leinster 11 clubs with 168 boats; in the lesser-populated Munster,

5 clubs with 28 boats, and finally Connaught, 2 clubs and 21 boats. This totals 34 clubs and 387 boats in the whole of Ireland, with the largest fleet at Ballyholme Y.C. where there were 45 boats. eight other clubs had fleets of around 20 boats.

Gus Henry passed the Chairman's office to Peter Duffy in 1974, and thereafter John McRobert from Ballyronan B.C. took over in 1976. Pat Murphy had started Dinghy Supplies and it was to become one of Ireland's leading dinghy equipment retailers and was immensely influential in assisting the development of the GP.

The 'troubles' in the north presented little, if any, obstacle to the operation of the Class, but they led to the International Association deciding, very reluctantly, not to return to Ballyholme for its 1973 event. The Irish Association mounted a campaign to have a major Class event come to Ireland and in 1977 the World Championship was hosted by Clontarf Y.& B.C in Dublin Bay when 80 boats participated.

By this stage in the development of the Class in Ireland many of the organisational structures and policies were well established and the committee spent more time on refining ideas, rather than creating new ones.

One such was the introduction of the Gold, Silver, and Bronze Leagues which was introduced in 1978. This was an attempt to spread the prizes more throughout the fleet and to motivate less experienced sailors to improve their sailing.

The 25th anniversary celebration of the Class in Ireland was driven forward by Pat Murphy who became Chairman in 1979. Skerries S.C. was invited to host the event as part of the Autumn Open Meeting and enjoyed what was probably the highest attendance at a domestic event ever, before or since, when 92 boats competed.

The aprés-sail was great fun with the anniversary dinner in the clubhouse where Bill Whisker (in drag) presented a memento to Ernie Mawhinney for his contribution to the Class over 25 years.

A decision to extend the racing season later into the year was taken in 1981 when it was agreed to hold a late Autumn Open Meeting. It was not until 1985 that this was re-christened the more enticing sounding Hot Toddy.

In 1982 the Championship of Ireland went to Lough Erne Y.C. and this turned out to be one of the more memorable events in its history.

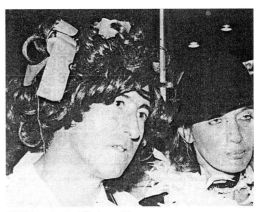

Bill Whisker (on the left) winner of the 25th Anniversary Meeting, looking almost as pretty as Rosemary, in drag at the Anniversary Dinner

Around that time the social aspect of major events had various of the more extrovert members prepared to don fancy dress and put on skits which played on the eccentricities of all and sundry. Among other items the mob from East Antrim B.C. produced a highly amusing version of 'the Owl and the Pussycat' featuring Melanie Morris' pea green optimist!

Throughout the late 70s and early 80s the committee minutes record many references to weight control of the boats. Obeche timber had become fashionable and everyone wanted his or her boat down to the minimum weight. This tended to create suspicions that some competitors, none in Ireland, it must be pointed out, were not above the use of illegal correctors!! Clearly, this generated more heat than light, and we doubt if every Irish sailor has absolutely clean hands!

In 1982 the top role in the Irish Association changed its name from Chairman to President, and Curly Morris became the first holder. As the 80s progressed the growth in GPs started to flatten and there is some evidence of a drop in attendances at Open Events. Whereas in the 60s and 70s the Irish sailors tended to go to Britain for Championships, there is clear indication of the traffic increasingly being in the other direction as we go through the 80s into the 90s.

Norman Lee from Dun Laoghaire M.Y.C. followed Curly Morris as President in 1984 and he was succeeded in turn by Tom Jobling from East Antrim B.C. in 1986. Tom has a well earned reputation as someone who is always on the lookout for new ideas, and it was during his time as President that the scope of the Junior Championship was widened in 1987 to become the Youth Championship, incorporating the junior event. Perhaps as a recognition of the maturity of the fleet, 1989 saw the introduction of the Masters' Championship.

Ireland's second opportunity to host the World Championship came in 1988 when Howth Y.C. ran an excellent event which attracted 138 entries. The event was marked by strong winds and a liberal supply of Heineken lager. The new Irish Honorary Secretary, Joe Martin agreed to crew with the Honorary Treasurer of the International Association, John Hunter, who was a consummate river sailor. After their first race capsize, some of Joe's friends remarked that he was very obliging to help John out. After their second race capsize with two gyrations, Joe's friends thought he was very charitable. On the third day's capsize of monstrous proportions, Joe's friends were convinced he was in need of psychiatric treatment!

Joe Martin (right), Irish Association Secretary, shares a joke with Joe Crilly

A gradual decline

Another Dun Laoghaire sailor, John Delap, became President in 1988 and in 1992 he in turn was followed by Robert Gingles of East Antrim B.C. The impact of more and more cruisers and the growth of marinas meant that dinghy sailing was facing real competition for newcomers to the sport. New, lightweight, dinghy designs were drawing off some of those younger people who might otherwise have moved into GPs and the Irish GP Class began to experience a gradual decline in boats on the water, and people prepared to contribute to the success of the Class. Fortunately, however, as a design the GP is robust, and if looked after, boats can last a long time and there are lots of perfectly sound used boats around. This, together with a well-run Class Association continued to offer the value for money factor which was missing in many competing equations

After Robert Gingles came Sutton D.C.'s Riocard O'Tiarnaigh in 1992. Riocard is a big personality and had very determined views on how to develop the Class. As a former educationalist, he recognised that training was vital in helping new people get to grips with the sport, so he organised seminars. He also identified the need to promote the Class and encouraged the International Association to bring the British Inland Championship to Lough Erne Y.C. in 1994.

Riocard, together with Tom Jobling and Paul Rowan came together in 1995 to promote the 40th Celebration Championship and classic regatta at Newtownabbey B.C., the original home of the GP. It was in the loft of Ernie Crawford's home at Greenisland, now owned by Paul Rowan, that three of the earliest GPs, numbers 374, 375 and 376 were built, and from whose slipway they were sailed.

Above: The first Irish boat nears completion at 33 Shore Road, Greenisland. Harold Crawford surveys his new toy
Inset: The 'Factory' at Clevedon House, 33 Shore Road

The event, which was blessed with Mediterranean type weather, attracted 83 boats and a wonderful cross section of the personalities in the Class over the 40 years. The oldest boat was GP 374, resplendent with wooden mast and boom, and cotton sails as originally rigged, and the newest was GP 13413. The youngest competitor was 17 year old Gemma Healy and the eldest, 82 year old Jim McLeod, both from Sligo.

Tom Jobling with Peter Duffy (right) - overheated at the Classic Regatta in Newton Abbey, 1995

Tom Jobling's immense contribution to the ruby celebration was to produce a memento Handbook for the occasion called 'Reflections of a General Purpose Nature'. This was a quite unsurpassed series of beautifully written articles, great photos and lists of winners chronicling the GP and its members in Ireland over the years, and many of those who attended the celebrations still enjoy reading their copy. Indeed, this chapter owes much to Tom's efforts.

A grand celebratory dinner in the main hall of the adjacent University of Ulster attended by 290 members and friends saw Ernie Mawhinney awarded Honorary Life Membership of the Association. Many amusing anecdotes ranging back to the earliest days were told by the likes of Bill Whisker, back from Australia, Ronnie Nichol, Pat Murphy and Riocard O'Tiarnaigh.

The frequent visits to Ireland of great competitors like Richard Estaugh and Simon Relph meant that Irish sailors did not achieve the recognition they might otherwise have done, and this was a constant source of concern to Brendan Kennedy, who sailed with Ken Louden at Lough Foyle Y.C. Unhappily Brendan passed away in 1994 and his wife, Isobella, at the 40th Celebration event, presented a beautifully designed trophy to be awarded to the highest placed Irish boat in the Championship of Ireland. The first winners were Hugh Gill and Stephen Boyle of Sutton D.C.

Riocard, and long serving Honorary Secretary, Joe Martin, played a crucial part in attracting the 1997 World Championship to Ireland, this time to Skerries S.C., the venue for many successful GP events over the years. Skerries put on a great show with an excellent blend of good racing, easily available refreshments and fun social events. Their reward was the best entry ever in a GP event in Ireland of 140 boats, which exceeded turnouts for other major GP Championships around that era.

Shortly after the end of the Skerries event, Riocard became the third person to be elected President of the International Association, an honour he had earned through the application of a great deal of creative energy on behalf of GP sailors.

Clive Brandon of Lough Foyle Y.C. became Irish President in 1995 after Riocard and during his term the Class produced another innovation. This was the GP Challenge in 1998, which had a unique format of fleet racing on the Saturday where the 32 competitors raced in small groups of 4 boats, leading on the Sunday to a knockout format where the last two surviving boats entered a match racing competition. The venue for the Challenge was the Broadmeadows at Malahide under the burgee of Swords S.& B.C., and provided excellent spectator entertainment, quite apart from the fun had by those competing.

There are 235 boats recorded in the 2000 Handbook of the Association spread over 24 clubs. While many clubs have seen a decline in boat numbers, and some have disappeared from the list, a few have maintained or increased their fleets. Clubs like Sligo Y.C. and Newtownards S.C. are testimony to the power of enthusiasm and commitment on the part of Fleet Captains and other stalwarts of the Class.

The new millennium started with John McGuinness as President. John sails with brother Donal at the most northerly club in Ireland, Moville B.C., only a few miles from Malin Head. At the A.G.M. in August it is expected that Ireland will break new ground in the GP world by achieving the election of its first lady President, Fionnula Burke, or Byrne as most GP people know her. Not before time!

The 'top guns'

It is impossible to adequately summarise the 'whose who?' of GP racing in Ireland, so let us concentrate on the premier event of the seven Class Championships and Open Meetings per season. From 1956 to 1969 the event was known as the Northern Ireland Championship, and thereafter as the Championship of Ireland.

Until the early 80s the event was largely a domestic contest, but from then on the impact of some of the top sailors from Britain involved with the trade became very evident.

Undoubtedly the name of Bill Whisker stands out. Even though he spent four years in Canada in the 60s and finally emigrated to Australia in 1981, Bill, first with Tim McMillan, followed by a lengthy spell with Jimmie McKee and finally with Bryan Willis, won the Championship no less than nine times. Up to 1980 other multi-winners were Ernie Mawhinney (3 times) with Milton Farmer and Ronnie Nichol, Burton Allen (2) with Issu Duffy, Curly Morris (4) with Tommy Hutcheson, Tom Jobling and twice with wife Ann, Paul Rowan (2) with Graham Gingles, and Peter Duffy (2) with John Nixon and Tom Jobling.

In the second half of the 50 years, the winners were more spread. Simon Relph stands out having won the Championship on six occasions until injury slowed him down, and Richard Estaugh on three. Among the Irish sailors, Mark and Paul Fekkes either won or were runners-up to a GB sailor on three occasions, Hugh Gill (2) with Stephen Boyle, and Curly Morris (2) with Ann.

Looking at all the Championship winners or Irish runners-up by club, East Antrim BC came out tops with fifteen wins, just pipping Ballyholme YC's thirteen wins. Ballyholme's successes were more in the first quarter century, whereas East Antrim BC's wins were spread throughout the 50 years. Thereafter the record shows Newtownabbey BC (4), Clontarf Y&BC (3), and Sutton DC (2). So the top club, in terms of its members pot hunting, has to be East Antrim BC.

See Addendum at the end of this chapter.

Crews' Union

Digging around in the archives produced an interesting document entitled 'GP14 Crews and the GP Association' which played on the emotions of your average GP crew with the following emotive pleas:

- *Fed up listening to the smart Alec at the back of the boat quoting from one of his three editions per year of Mainsail dedicated to crewing, helming, tuning and looking after the geep?*

- *Want to avoid having to beg smart Alec for a look at one of his copies of Mastgate?*

- *Like to see your name up in lights in the Class Handbook along with his nibs, and have all the latest details of Class developments and records of the placings in major Championships (in which you would have finished higher except smart Alec kept tacking off the lifts and hanging on in the headers)?*

- *Think that 50% of the GP (wo)manpower ought to have more voice in the Association's affairs?*

Right

- *Join the GP Association as an Associate Member*

Needless to say family relationships have come under scrutiny from time to time. Ken Heskin wrote in 1982 under the title 'That's no lady, that's my crew', about sailing with his wife Sue:

What I am talking about is the transition that occasionally takes place in both of us from doting spouses to spouting doses (of abuse) once afloat. In these exchanges, I tend to be the somewhat more voluble and sarcastic partner but Sue wins on malicious persistence, although capable of the more terse and pithy wit!

An interchange will usually begin by my exercising the God-given right of any helm to comment (constructively) on the crew's performance. Hence, rounding the leeward mark, I might say "Sue, I am all for the crew using initiative, but we'd probably better get the spinnaker down before the weather mark". Sue normally responds to this sort of observation by invoking the crew's God-given right to cripple the helm with the spinnaker pole and point out that I am standing on the spinnaker halyard - thus adding insult to injury! Invariably, of course, I am not standing on it - it just happens to be wrapped around my ankle!

Anyone recognise the scene?

So there is some evidence that a Crews' Union in Ireland was needed, and once set up, has long been a powerful influence on the way things get done. Not satisfied with demanding padded toestraps, soft feel genoa sheets, and the rest, the union leadership demanded that its members could turn up 5 minutes before the time to go afloat, and were to be provided with 2 glasses of their favourite tipple within 15 minutes of coming ashore!

Needless to say, it is not difficult to see why many helms seem to spend far too much of their time in the dinghy park while crews can be seen propping up the bar and being the centre of the social scene! Over the years some of the more notorious - sorry personable - crews have driven Ireland's determination that going to a GP weekend has to be fun for both sailors and friends alike.

Huge personalities like Ronnie Nichol the quiet man, the wryly humoured Bertie Forsythe, the late and greatly loved first Chairman of the Crews' Union, Ciaran Byrne, the 'Bohemian' Graham 'Gingy' Gingles who enjoyed as much success with the ladies as he did in his sailing, big Jimmie McKee from Donaghadee, Niall Henry for his dramatic skills, the determined Fionnula Byrne and 'spin doctor' Padraig Smith who now sail together, the incredibly eccentric Chris Penny, the massively extrovert Issu Duffy, and the charming Charlotte O'Tiarnaigh.

There is a great tale about the 1974 Championship of Ireland at Lough Swilly when Pat Murphy was cajoled into 'baptising' the abstemious Jimmie McKee by pouring a pint of beer over his head. The holy spirit evoked an immediate response from Jimmie which floored Pat!

Signposts to the best craic

Irish sailors like to think that the racing is not a matter of life and death, and only the social side is more important than that! Racing has always been keenly contested, but an event is not rated unless it is judged to have been 'great craic'. Over the years some venues have been particularly popular, or have hosted notable events.

Ireland is truly blessed with a surfeit of marvellous dinghy Championship locations from sea venues such as Lough Swilly or Sligo Bay, Larne Lough or Belfast Lough, Strangford Lough or Carlingford Lough, Skerries or Howth, Dublin Bay or Bray, Cork Harbour as well as any number of other less populated locations in the south and west. Alternatively, there are excellent inland water spots such as Lough Neagh or Lough Erne, Lough Ennel at Mullingar or the vast Shannon waterway, the Broadmeadows near Dublin or Blessington Lake in the Wicklow mountains.

There are also some very talented organisers of sailing events in Ireland, and competitors are well able to identify the crucial factors that make the difference. From time to time, however, events come along which are built round a good idea that catches the imagination, and that can make a significant difference to the attendance.

Readers will no doubt be thinking that any assessment of the merits of a venue will be entirely subjective, which is wrong - well partly wrong! However, it is said that people vote with their feet, and the Irish Association's statistician has incontrovertible numeric data to prove the point, by way of numbers supporting each event. Our analysis may prove surprising to some when they discover that GP sailors prefer organisation over opulence, friendliness over familiarity, and the craic factor over the cost equation. That's not to say that they don't expect good value for money, because they are very quick to spot a rip-off!

Over the years the best attended events on the east coast were consistently at Skerries, Sutton and Blessington, all of which have good indigenous fleets. In the north, Newtownabbey, boosted by the Ruby Championship, Newtownards and East Antrim. In the west, as might be expected, the holiday venues of Sligo and Lough Erne attracted consistent support.

It is not all upside, however. In the province of Munster, support for the GP has rather come and gone over the years. Around the mid-90s there was a significant revival of interest in Cork Harbour and the 1996 Championship of Ireland at Royal Cork YC attracted 64 entries. Since then, there has been a significant falling away of interest which is very disquieting.

Looking outward

So much for inward reflection on the GP scene in Ireland, but Irish members have played their part in supporting and developing the activities of the Association around the world. Things like hosting major events for the International Association in Ireland, supporting events in GB and further afield, and playing their part in the organisation of the affairs of the Association.

In 1963 a group of GP sailors decided to attend the British National Championship at Llandudno in North Wales. Six boats were shipped on the Belfast-Liverpool ferry and conveyed by freight train to Llandudno. Quite apart from the logistical difficulties of getting to the event the Irish sailors were initially overawed by the huge number of 140 boats parked round the promenade. However, they quickly seemed to have recovered their composure because besides Burton Allen finishing 2nd and Bill Whisker 4th, all 6 boats ended in the top 25. Part of this unexpected success may have been to do with the Irish expertise in handling the spinnaker which had been introduced in 1962, as there are stories of other competitors being overtaken to leeward by superb spinnaker handling!

Buoyed up by their Llandudno success and having invested in some double stackers a further foray across the Irish sea took place in 1965 when eleven boats went to Helensburgh for the British Nationals. This time no mistakes were made and after a great bit of sailing in GP 6007, Burton Allen, crewed by Issu Duffy were convincing winners with two firsts, a second, third and a fourth. Frank Chapman, a famous national journalist, wrote:

'There is no blarney required to describe the feat of Irish helmsmen in our National Championship sailed at Helensburgh S.C. Less than a dozen boats crossed the Irish sea to join the fleet of 108 and when the overall points were worked out it was revealed that four of them finished in the top ten'.

Irish pot hunters at Helensburgh in 1965

A halcyon era

This was the start of a halcyon era for GP's generally and for Irish success 'across the water' against the old enemy. The 'Irish team' went to Torquay in 1966 with great support from Graham Chambers' fine 45 ft cruiser 'Glance' which was used as team support boat. After racing ,everyone adjourned back to Glance where Graham and Nan had refreshments like scones, or sometimes cream buns, and tea ready

'Glance' - support vessel to the Irish GP team in the 1960's - seen here with 'Ventura'

and waiting. Once again, Burton and Issu shone, but they failed to win the event by a single point, and Curly Morris accepts full responsibility! Curly tells it this way:

"I had been experiencing a series of broken rudder blades, and had taken the precaution of carrying a spare blade in the boat. In the final race, when lying 2nd across the first reach, the blade broke. We managed to prevent the boat capsizing, and I changed the blade in record time, eventually finishing 6th just ahead of Burton. Had we retired when the blade broke, Burton might have gained the extra point he needed to retain the title."

In 1968 the Championship returned to Llandudno and 6 Irish boats took part. While Burton Allen was missing, Paul Rowan and Graham Gingles kept up the record of Irish success by taking the runner-up spot in what was a strong wind event. John McWilliam, by now a Flight Lieutenant in the R.A.F. raced GP 4441 'Cymyran', an old R.A.F. S.C. boat and won the second race, but otherwise had undistinguished results.

Things were to be different the following year, 1968, when the British Championship went to Thorpe Bay Y.C. in Essex. The fleet of 142 boats again encountered mostly strong and cold conditions, and the competition was to turn into a two horse race between the clubmates from Larne, John McWilliam and Paul Rowan, who had sailed in the former's GP in the late 50s. Paul, again with Graham Gingles, had the use of Michael Hill's very fast GP 7442, 'Trostan', and won the first two races with John McWilliam and John Patterson, second on both occasions. The two Johns in 'Cymyran' reversed the position by winning the third race with 'Trostan' second.

In the fourth race, the kicker bracket on the mast failed while 'Trostan' was leading the race, letting 'Cymyran' go on to win the race, only to be disqualified in the post-race scrutineering when the centreboard failed to measure. It was all to play for in the final race which was in lighter winds. John McWilliam secured his third win, and the Championship, while Paul Rowan could only manage fourth, making him runner-up for the second year.

By the middle 60s the Irish had stamped their personality successfully on the GP scene in Britain and with the influence brought to bear by Ken Dunlop, as President of the International Association, the British Championship was to cross the Irish Sea to Ballyholme Y.C. in 1969. In terms of the Irish record of successes over the previous four years another local winner might have been anticipated. It was not to be. While Peter Duffy was fourth overall and there were four Irish boats in the first nine, the winner was fellow Celt, Peter Curry from the Kyles of Bute S.C. who dominated the fleet.

Major events in Britain continued to attract groups of Irish boats, but the top of the fleet dominance of the mid-60s did not continue, although individuals did achieve good results. Peter Duffy was fourth at Plymouth in 1970, John McWilliam third in the second World Championship in 1971 at Thorpe Bay, and Paul Rowan and Peter Duffy were second and third at Helensburgh in 1973, while Curly Morris did best in 1974 when he was third at Thorpe Bay.

'Whiskee Too' - with Bill Whisker and Jimmie McKee, World Champions in 1975

World Championship success

Ireland's next great success was at the 1975 World Championship at Stone Harbour, New Jersey, U.S.A. The Irish have been represented at all the GP Worlds, and have usually sent at least one, and more often, two container loads of boats. Bill Whisker, who was skilled at getting to grips quickly with new sailing waters, crewed by Jimmie McKee dominated the event by winning three races and comfortably assigning Eddie Warden-Owen, who later became a well-known professional sailor, to the runner-up spot.

Success eluded the Irish for some years until 1979 when Bill Whisker, now with Bryan Willis, was pipped from retaining his title by the new kid on the block, Richard Estaugh. Bill and Bryan went on to be third in the British Championship at Llandudno later in 1979.

For reasons that are not easily identifiable the enthusiasm of Irish sailors to attend the British Championship waned noticeably in the 80s. Possibly one reason was that the Irish found the social side of events becoming too stereotyped, whereas there seemed to be more craic at events in Ireland, and this in turn attracted regular support from Britain.

One exception to this was the Mumbles World Championship of 1985 which attracted the largest ever Worlds' fleet of an incredible 196 boats. Bearing in mind that a trio of 'super Champs', Simon Relph, Neil Marsden and Richard Estaugh took the first three places in the Championship, the fifth overall by Paul Rowan and Mark Nolan was creditable.

Howth Y.C. had the honour of hosting the 1988 World Championship which attracted 141 competitors. Best of the Irish sailors were the up and coming team of brothers Mark and Paul Fekkes from East Antrim B.C. who ended seventh. Three years later the Fekkes brothers took a giant leap forward when they, together with fifteen other crews from Ireland, went to Cape May, New Jersey, U.S.A. for the 1991 Worlds.

Racing against the likes of Richard Estaugh, Ian Willis and Simon Relph, Mark and Paul put on an expert display of competitive sailing which included two firsts, a second and a third, to win impressively Ireland's second World Championship title.

Major success for Irish sailors in World or British Championships proved elusive in the 90s. Why this should be is anyone's guess, but a slightly less competitive domestic racing scene may possibly account for it.

Nonetheless, Skerries S.C. proved to be excellent hosts for the World Championship in 1997 which attracted very good support at 141 boats. The club put on an excellent show all round, and especially in the social and catering arrangements.

And so to the present year when, in April, the World Championship 2000 was held in Durban, South Africa. Once again Ireland supported the event with 14 boats out of a fleet of 59, and some of the Irish competitive magic returned. Damien Bracken and Alan Parker of Clontarf Y.&.B.C. were third and Ruan O'Tiarnaigh and Stephen Boyle fourth. Six Irish boats finished in the top fourteen. Crowning the results was Andy Thompson of East Antrim B.C.'s achievement of helping Richard Estaugh to win the event

Champion of champions

Okay Amigo! - Issu and Peter Duffy with the Helmsman's Championship Trophy in 1974

This record of GP competitive success would be incomplete without a mention of the I.S.A.'s Helmsman's Championship of Ireland. Over the years the GP from 1959 to 1995 has been selected Class in which the event was held. This is a tribute to the qualities of the boat as one which offered the possibility of the organisers finding sixteen boats of similar competitive standard.

All the major Classes in Ireland are invited annually to nominate the highest placed Irish sailor in their Class Championship, and all the Class Champions race against other to discover the Champion of Champions. Over the years the following GP sailors have won the title:

1967	Curly Morris	East Antrim B.C.	Sailed in GP14s	
1974	Peter Duffy	Ballyholme Y.C.	Sailed in GP14s	
1980	Bill Whisker	Ballyholme Y.C.	Sailed in GP14s	National 18s
1984	Paul Rowan	Newtownabbey B.C.	Sailed in GP14s	
1985	Paul Rowan	Newtownabbey B.C.	Sailed in GP14s	National 18s
1995	Ruan O'Tiarnaigh	Sutton D.C.	Sailed in GP14s	

The GP Class in Ireland presented the 'GP14 First Time Helm Trophy' to the I.S.A. in 1993 to be awarded to the highest placed helm participating for the first time.

D.I.Y and the Professionals

As you can read elsewhere in this book the role of Bell Woodworking kits played a major part in the early growth of the GP Class. Aside of that, groups of handy people were doing their own thing building GPs from the plans. Some of these boats were well over weight and proved to be uncompetitive, and in occasional cases, did not measure. The Bell kits put some quality control into the D.I.Y. process and they made it possible to produce consistent boats.

However, there were always some people who were prepared to pay to have their GPs professionally built. In Ireland in the late 50s that service was provided by a second generation family-run building company called Samuel Duffin Ltd. which operated from modest premises almost in the shadow of Goliath cranes of Belfast shipbuilders, Harland & Wolff. Gerry Duffin was a member of Holywood Y.C., just across Belfast Lough from North Belfast Y.C., and aside of building work, he built the occasional clinker-construction boat. In 1958, Gerry built himself a GP, and for the next ten years or so, produced one or two boats per year gradually increasing to around six.

In the mid-60s, Gerry Duffin sent one of his sons, Alistair, to train as a cabinet-maker with one of Belfast's foremost timber importers and joinery companies, J.P.Corry Ltd. With his training completed, young Alistair joined the family business in 1968 and helped build the GPs. Almost at the same time, however, the Duffin GP faced competition locally.

This came about in an unlikely way. Over the winter of 1967-68 Michael Hill had built his second boat, the famous 'Trostan', GP 7442, using ideas he had come across when he sailed 505s. Michael created a new profile for the boat by giving her a rounded foredeck, minimum rocker and flattened aft-sections. Michael also employed an incredible amount of pre-bend (for that era) in setting up the metal mast which had only just been allowed in the Class.

Trostan at Thorpe Bay in 1968 - note the mast bend

Michael Hill loaned 'Trostan' to Paul Rowan to compete in the 1968 British Championship at Thorpe Bay, and so impressed was Paul that he decided to have built a GP with similar characteristics. So he turned to a local Scorpion Class builder, Trevor Stewart, who produced well-built, attractive looking, and successful dinghies. Thereafter, Trevor built a number of GPs which proved very competitive, including 'Whiskee Too', the boat in which Bill

Whisker and Jimmie McKee won many competitions. Sad to say, in the mid-70s, after a short illness, Trevor passed away and this robbed Ireland of a fine craftsman and dinghy sailor.

Many of the readers of this book will not be aware that glass fibre GPs were manufactured in Ireland. In 1971, the Irish Association agreed, following advice from Ken Dunlop, representing the International Association, to grant a G.R.P. manufacturing licence to McComb Plastics of Lisburn, Co. Antrim. Headed by Rodney McComb and directed technically by Royal Ulster Y.C. member, Bob Hutchinson, the company manufactured a range of pleasure craft, and, as part of an expansion into the manufacture of the Ruffian range of yachts, Bill Whisker was recruited into the marine business. Bill's knowledge, enthusiasm and network resulted in increased demand for an improving product, and McCombs transferred production to a tailor-made facility near Newtownards. A small team which included Larne's Tom Jobling and Johnny Mullan from Ballyholme produced a number of successful GPs. G.R.P. boats have not, until recently, been greatly sought after by Irish GP sailors who, instead, preferred the work of the cabinet makers, and McCombs ceased manufacturing GPs in 1975.

Besides boat builders, GP sailors in Ireland could buy sails from Tasker Sails Ireland based in Crosshaven, Co. Cork. John McWilliam, who on leaving the R.A.F., went to Hong Kong to train as a sailmaker with Rolly Tasker, set up this sailmaking business. John only produced GP sails for a short time in the early 70s before orientating the business towards big boats, and eventually re-branding it as McWilliam Sailmakers.

The boat that Jack built.....Alistair developed

Alistair Duffin has played an immense part in the subsequent development of the GP. In 1995, at the Ruby Celebrations, it was striking to compare the extent of the changes which have taken place to the deck and interior of the boat which were evident by comparing GP 374, in its almost original condition, with some of the most then Series II wooden boats in the 13,300 range. This modernisation of the design has been achieved without any change to the external hull dimensions or overall weight.

Even though he was only out of his apprenticeship as a cabinet maker in the late 60s, Alistair was stung by the move of some GP sailors to order boats from Trevor Stewart, and he resolved to improve the Duffin product. At the time his hobby was motorcycling, but by the early 70s he had decided he should build himself a GP and go sailing, which brought him into closer contact with the fleet.

Alistair changed the method of the rounding of the foredeck from that on boats produced by Trevor Stewart. Then spruce was replaced by obeche, comfort strips were introduced to aid sitting out, a front bulkhead shelf was introduced, underfloor control lines, maximum /minimum rubbing strakes, and all the while continually improving the aesthetic appearance of the GP by way of the use of inserts in the deck, thwart and sidebenches.

Alistair Duffin with Chris Penny

In the late 80s the International Association, under the guidance of industrial designers, Nick Colbourne and David Rowlands, began to think about developing a GP which would have no need for self-bailers and sidetanks intruding into the cockpit. Two development projects were set in train, one of which was undertaken by Alistair Duffin with a free hand to build the boat as he saw fit. When the two prototypes were evaluated, the Duffin version with its flatter inner floor seemed to meet the Class needs better and became accepted as the Series II which was approved in the early 90s.

Not content with the Series II, which of course still required self-bailers to a limited degree, and also tended to float too high on its side while capsized, in 1998 Alistair persuaded Ireland's Chief Measurer, Jimmie McKee to promote the idea of a further development. The thrust of this would do away with the need for self-bailers, correct the problem of excess side buoyancy, and remove the washboards which would then be redundant. The International Association agreed to Alistair's suggestion and added the thought that he should also investigate through the deck sheeting for the genoa.

Working with Ralph Chadwick, the Chairman of the Technical and Rules Sub-Committee, a prototype has been constructed and is being raced by Alistair in Ireland as part of an evaluation process. So far, the modifications appear to meet the development criteria, and the deck appearance of the boat is very clean. One of the hidden benefits to what, in due course, might become known as the Series III, is a not insignificant saving in cost. All being well, the prototype will appear at Southport for the 50th Anniversary celebrations.

Putting something back

Part of the strength of the GP Association in Ireland has been the willingness of its members to contribute to the organisation of the Class activities, not only in Ireland, but as members of the International Association Committee.

Ireland has supplied three Presidents of the International Association over the 50 years, Ken Dunlop. Paul Rowan and our current President, Riocard O'Tiarnaigh. Each brought their individual interests and strengths to bear on the Association, but perhaps they all had one common characteristic, in that they were not afraid to promote new ideas while respecting the best traditions of the Class.

Over the years, also, the Irish Association, due to its proximity to Crewe, has been able to have its President and Honorary Secretary attend committee meetings of the International Association. This has brought the two parts of the Association closer together, created many and lasting friendships, and, we believe, has been of crucial benefit to the development of the Class.

GP sailors have also made a major contribution to the sport of sailing in Ireland through their involvement with the Irish Sailing Association in one or other of its guises over the past 40 years. Clive Brandon, Hugh Gill, Peter Hannon, Gus Henry, Ken Heskin, Joe Martin, Curly Morris, and Paul Rowan have all played their part on I.S.A. committees. Padraig Boyle and Riocard O'Tiarnaigh served on the I.S.A. Council.

In Ulster, too many to mention GP sailors have represented their clubs on the R.Y.A. Northern Ireland Council. In the past Michael Hill has been the Chairman of the Council, and the present holder of the office is Curly Morris, who has the support of seven present or former GP sailors on his committee.

Ireland's contribution

Irish sailors have had over the years, and will continue to have, great fun through their involvement with GPs over the years. They have been influential in the technical, administrative, and social development of the Class and will, no doubt, continue to play their part in the future.

And Finally...

In 1980, the week-long Championship of Ireland at Larne was well sponsored by the Bank of Ireland. Each day there was a prize-giving where helms and crews of the leading 3 boats were presented with cut-glass whisky tumblers. Now there were 2 youthful teams from Britain doing much of the winning. After the presentation, the tumblers would be filled with Black Bush and eventually taken back to their lodgings. Their landlady could not understand where these expensive glasses were coming from (had they been 'lifted' ?, was her idea) and decided that she would keep them safe until the end of the week. Of course, Richard Estaugh and Bob Talboys, Adrian Kneen and Linus Birtles were there to take all they could get, but only on the water!

GP14 CLASS CHAMPIONSHIP OF IRELAND ADDENDUM
(Incorporating the Northern Ireland Championship 1956 - 1969)

YEAR	BOAT	HELM	CREW	VENUE
1956	796	Ernie Mawhinney	Milton Farmer	County Antrim Y.C
1957	796	Ernie Mawhinney	Milton Farmer	County Antrim Y.C.
1958	1948	Beattie Purcell	Miara Purcell	Quoile Y.C.
1959	1314	John McWilliam	Victor Poots	Larne Y.C.
1960	2006	Hugh Kennedy	Joe Kennedy	Ballyholme Y.C.
1961	2759	Burton Allen	not known	Carrickfergus S.C.
1962	1787	Bill Whisker	Tim McMillan	County Antrim Y.C.
1963	1787	Bill Whisker	Tim McMillan	East Antrim B.C.
1964	3772	Curly Morris	Tommy Hutcheson	Killyleagh Y.C.
1965	3613	Paul Rowan	Graham Gingles	Ballyholme Y.C.
1966	6007	Burton Allen	Issu Duffy	Carrickfergus S.C.
1967	3772	Curly Morris	Tom Jobling	East Antrim B.C.
1968	796	Ernie Mawhinney	Ronnie Nichol	Killyleagh Y.C.
1969	7442	Michael Hill	Charlie Lynch	Sligo Y.C.
1970	8138	Peter Duffy	John Nixon	Ballyholme Y.C.
1971	8351	Paul Rowan	Graham Gingles	Sligo Y.C.
1972	8138	Peter Duffy	Tom Jobling	Wexford S.C.
1973	9793	Bill Whisker	Jimmie McKee	Ballyholme Y.C.
1974	10845	Bill Whisker	Jimmie McKee	Lough Swilly Y.C.
1975	10111	Pat Murphy	Ciaran Byrne	Fenit S.C.
1976	3772	Curly Morris	Ann Morris	Skerries S.C.
1977	10669	Malcolm Crone	Brian Jess	East Down Y.C.
1978	10111	Pat Murphy	Ciaran Byrne	Lough Swilly Y.C.
1979	11700	Bill Whisker	Bryan Willis	Baltimore S.C.
1980	12066	Richard Estaugh	Bob Talboys	East Antrim B.C.
1981	12250	Bill Whisker	Bryan Willis	Malahide S.C.
1982	12217	Simon Relph	Colin Deighon	Lough Erne Y.C.
1983	11669	Curly Morris	Ann Morris	Galway Bay B.C.
1984	12594	Simon Relph	Justin Chisholm	East Down Y.C.
1985	12594	Simon Relph	Andy Service	Sligo Y.C.
1986	10900	Robert Gingles	Paul Fekkes	East Antrim B.C.
1987	12817	Simon Relph	Andy Service	Wexford S.C.
1988	12743	John Lavery	Mark Nolan	Blessington S.C.
1989	12521	Mark Fekkes	Paul Fekkes	Lough Erne Y.C.
1990	12988	Simon Relph	Tom Hall	Sligo Y.C.
1991	13123	Mark Fekkes	Paul Fekkes	East Down Y.C.
1992	13188	Simon Relph	Mark Platt	Skerries S.C.
1993	13177	Hugh Gill	Stephen Boyle	Newtownards S.C.
1994	13177	Hugh Gill	Stephen Boyle	Cove S.C.
1995	13377	Richard Estaugh	Brian O'Hara	Newtownabbey B.C.
1996	13479	Richard Estaugh	Simon Potts	Royal Cork Y.C.
1997	13314	David Fletcher	Barry Jobling	Newtownards S.C.
1998	13583	Damian Bracken	Allen Parker	Sligo Y.C.
1999	13654	Neil Marsden	Derek Hill	East Antrim B.C.

A Western Australian Perspective

Desert Crossing Christmas Day 1968

1960's. As in many other aspects of Australian life, migrants play a large part in changing and enriching the leisure time spent by 'the man in the street'. Several GP's were brought from England during the decade and one of them was GP14 'Makore' No. 575 sailed in New South Wales by Cliff Boocock. He was to remain in isolation for a long time as the only boat registered in that State, as was No. 3737 built in Hobart, Tasmania in 1960 - the earliest registered Australian built GP and number. Probably the first boat built in Australia was in Mandurah Western Australia in 1950, but she was never registered.

The first General Meeting of the Australian Association was held in Victoria on 23rd May 1962. One of these original members was Arthur Palmer, a tireless worker for the Association for many years and who, to this day, still takes an interest in things GP. By the following year the distribution of registered boats had grown to, Victoria 52, South Australia 7, Queensland, Western Australia and Tasmania one each. The Victorian officers of the GP14 Class Association handled all administration of Australian affairs, whilst remaining under the umbrella of the parent body in England. There arose areas of disagreement regarding the construction of the boats - the U.K. on the one hand being determined to ensure that all G.P's strictly conformed to the one design concept, whereas the Australian attitude at that time was that a boat had to be built using locally available materials and fittings. One example of this problem was the availability of a suitable mast section - a problem which was to continue for many years. Mast importation was out of the question due to the prohibitive price. Eventually after some years a section became available which was acceptable to the International Association. The first Australian boats had to be built with deck stepped masts as extrusions of 22 feet in length were not available.

There were many other problems, suffice to say that none of the 100 or so Victorian boats, including their GRP version, complied to the U.K. measurement rules. A softened approach on both sides may have saved the Class in Victoria but as it was no Victorian boats competed in the World Championships in Perth, Western Australia in 1979. A great pity.

The situation probably contributed to the demise of the Class in Victoria over the ensuing ten years. Some of the Australian modifications of the early 60's are now incorporated in the International Rules of the Class - 30 years later.

Meanwhile the Class secured a tenuous hold in South Australia and Western Australia. The first registered boat in W.A. was 5927 'Tintookie' built by Mike Igglesden in 1962 and was mentioned in a local newspaper article as destined to 'sail in lonesome dignity on the crowded Swan River' for almost two years. In 1964 a letter appeared in the 'West Australian' newspaper extolling the virtues of the GP14 written by a Pat Holmes who was looking for a local boat with GP features. This, combined with the display of 'Tintookie' on the Rolly Tasker stand at the 1964 Perth Boat Show set in motion the formation of the W.A.Branch on July 8th 1965. The boat owners, or potential owners, who formed this initial committee were:- Pat Holmes - Chairman, John Hughes - Secretary, Mike Altria - Treasurer, Brian Kemp -who had built his boat in New South Wales - Publicity Officer and Mike Igglesden - Measurer. Others present who were to become indispensable to the Association over the coming years were Ian Peck and Mary Igglesden. In 1979 Mary was to be awarded an Honorary Life Membership of the International Association for 'services

'Tintookie' Dec. 1965

rendered'. Three boats were built by local boat builder Laurie Chivers and the requisite number of boats to make up a racing fleet was thus formed. Mounts Bay Sailing Club became the preferred club to join and offered excellent racing facilities, although most of this fledgling fleet were not proficient enough to really welcome the prospect of racing! The first race to be held under the auspices of the W.A.Branch at Mounts Bay Sailing Club was held on 12th September 1965 and was probably won by 6450 'Melody' Ian Peck although no record of the results exists. This year also saw the adoption of the Australian Constitution.

So the years flew by. Kits were made to assist and encourage home building and by 1969 there were 26 boats in Western Australia. 1970 saw the first G.R.P. boats come off the mould - Thames Marine Mk.2 design and the Class really blossomed. A wonderful family feeling was prevalent and the 'picnic days' were very well attended - often more boats supported these events than the racing events held every other weekend. By 1970 there were 50 boats in W.A.

The 'tyranny of distance' was not a problem to the fleet in the 60's and 70's. Trips to regattas were made to Albany - a port 400 kilometres to the south of Perth; Geraldton - 400 kilometres to the north; various lakes; islands offshore; voyages off shore - Bunbury to Busselton. Every other year the National Championships were held, Chelsea Yacht Club (Melbourne) alternating with Mounts Bay Sailing Club (Perth). The four day 3,500 km journey was tackled by stalwarts of the Class (plus the children) - 400 kms of the road was then only a sandy track which made towing a dinghy an interesting exercise and lengths of carpet and sacking were a necessary covering to protect the hulls from

Redback' on the Swan River Perth W.A.

stone damage and bull dust. One memorable sail held in Melbourne was the 2nd heat of the 1976 National Championships in Port Phillip Bay, renowned for its sudden weather changes and its reputation was upheld towards the end of this race when a sudden westerly change, with breezes up to 60 knots, overtook the fleet. Most of the boats retired and the race was abandoned. Some boats, including the W.A. boat 'Karapyet', which was in the lead at the time, 'sailed' back to the beach under bare poles, surfing on the large build up of waves. 'Karapyet's' skipper, Ron Stigant, avoided disaster by utilising the technique of riding on the back of the waves, right into the beach. If the boats were sailed too slowly then the next wave would swallow them up, if sailed too fast they would broach on the breaking crest. A perfect example of the reason for the ability to lower sails on the water rule. An exciting afternoon but very destructive as many boats lost their masts, booms and broke other gear.

One long weekend a 'Cue Regatta' was held. The closest sailing water to Cue is probably 350 km. to the west, but a 4-wheel drive bus - no boats- took 14 GP'ers on an inland exploration of old gold mines, aboriginal caves and sites. The last night there was a downpour of rain ("it never rains here this time of the year") and we could have been happy to have our boats with us as we almost commenced floating down the creek bed in our waterproof floored tents.

1973 was the year in which a 24 hour marathon world distance record was attempted. November was selected as a time of good constant breezes. A team of four boats sailed in relays of one hour each and enjoyed the first 8 hours sailing in a southwest 18-20 knot breeze, giving rise to high hopes, but by 2 am. a flat calm existed and it was 6 am. before a 15 knot easterly came in - too late! It had been a great family experience, camping on the beach under a starlit sky, around a camp fire, each group awaited their turn for the 'changeover'.

Mention has been made of some of the Australian modifications made to the boat, the most radical of which was, and still is, the trapeze. Arguments raged prior to its introduction but it is now accepted that it makes the boat more family oriented with lighter crews being able to compete on a more equal footing with, say, all adult crews.

After a year in the U.K. attending various RYA courses a GP stalwart returned to Perth in 1975 and established a Sailing Centre for the Education Department. GP14s were the obvious choice for the centre and some of the original boats are still sailing in the centre. Since then hundreds of people have been taught to sail aboard these General Purpose dinghies, as of course, they have around the world. What a boat!.

In 1977 a new plug was meticulously made by a small group of members, funding for the project being made by obtaining a bank loan and from members subscribing to non interest bearing debentures. In the following year the first new MkIII boat came out of the mould formed from this plug. Some stimulus to the new boats construction was the looming World Championships which the Branch was to host in January 1979. One of these boats, No. 11856, finishing 5th in the Championships. Over the next few years 35 MkIII's were to emerge from this mould and new home built wooden boats were no longer the preferred option. Many of these glass hulls were supplied to members who installed the timber work - floorboards, rubbing strips, centre boards, rudders, thwarts and side benches. Few members chose a plywood deck for their GRP hulls.

Nationals, Victoria 1970

Mount's Bay Sailing Club 1970

W.A. skippers have sailed in World Championships in America, Wales, Scotland, England and Ireland -one way to enjoy large fleet sailing not available at home.

The World Championships of '79 saw the rise and fall of the Class in W.A. Only people who have been involved in such an undertaking have any idea of the work required in order to conduct an event of this magnitude. A dedicated small band of workers, it was generally agreed, made the series an outstanding success, both on and off the water. The downside of this accomplishment was that the Regatta Committee were 'burnt out' by the time the event was over and the Class took a downward turn from then on. It is only now showing signs of recovery.

Since there were only 42 boats entered for the World Series, aspects such as measuring and social events were able to be organised in an almost family atmosphere. The measuring, however, was not all sweetness and light as some of the top overseas entries (8 Irish boats in one 12m container and 5 in another from England) were found to be underweight, some had unauthorised fittings and oversized sails and so on. Competitors from Wales, U.S.A. and S. Africa used borrowed boats - never a satisfactory solution for serious racing. The accuracy of the beam balance weighing scales were questioned but were proved to be within the weight of a teaspoon in accuracy. One sailor suggested that the boats would weigh less in Australia than in the northern hemisphere. A few tempers were frayed but the whole programme was carried out in good humour and there were no protests whatsoever against class rules. In fact some rules were changed upon the return to the U.K.

The Australian Championship which was held in the week preceding the World's was virtually a preview of results to come with visitors gaining the first six places. Richard Estaugh and Bob Tallboys sailing 'Bruce' were the winners as they were to be in the following week. The first W.A. boat in the Worlds was 'Aeolus', sailed by Murray Rann who, with his brother Vic, earned a highly commendable 4th result, when it is considered many of the visiting fleet were skippers and crew of a very high almost professional standard and the WA. branch consisted of only approx. 20 boats of mostly family combinations.

The climax of the week was the Presentation Dinner in the company of the Governor of W.A. Sir Wallace and Lady Kyle. The display of trophies was truly magnificent and each competitor was presented with an engraved plaque as a memorial to a 'wonderful Championships'. The visiting crews were so appreciative of the great time that they had experienced at M.B.S.C. that they turned on a party to say thanks to the club and the Championship organisers.

By 1984 W.A. was the only state racing GPs and the fleets were very small. 1997 saw the building of the first Series 11 boat and a gradual revival of the Class. The future is by no means assured. The requirement is an entrepreneur with vision, and money! We have fantastic sailing water, an unparalleled climate, a very friendly group of sailors - half of them women - but we still need new boats.

One of the fantastic spin off's from sailing the GP is that the friendships made in the 1960's and onward are still as strong as ever. Folk who no longer sail the boat, for one reason or another, meet up for various functions and events and all agree that their time in GPs was one of the happiest times of their lives. Just great!

Mike Igglesden

Ed. Mike, ever modest, failed to mention - and I quote from the report from John Morris 25 years ago.

"Competition was keen but the final race saw Mike Igglesden in 'Merry Jest' with his crew Ray O'Neil take over the title for W.Australia. John Hughes sailing 'Kristin' with John Morris acting as forward hand took the runner-up position. So W.A. had their first National titles holder in Mike, a very popular winner in view of his having virtually started the Class in W.A."

'Casper' on the Swan River, Perth W.A.

Memories of Darkest Africa - 1950's

By Jim Gilmour, Bunbury W.A.

Aberdovey

I only sailed a couple of races there with Peter Morris (now deceased) as my career was interfering with my visits there in that period. I recall that GP1 was sailing and was told that Jack Holt was racing it, though I did not meet him. I went to Kenya soon after that (1950) so I have not seen Aberdovey again since (unfortunately, as it is a beautiful spot).

Kenya

The town of Kisumu is on the Kavirondo Gulf at the N.E.corner of Lake Victoria (second largest lake in the world). The gulf is about 60 miles long and several miles wide. What magnificent sailing. Regular winds - 5 to 15 knots and pretty consistent, starting at 10.45am on the clock each day till dusk.

At that stage the club was sailing very heavy pre-war dinghies (16ft long with 1/2in planking and small sail area - very slow - in my book, 'barges'). A couple of years after my arrival I travelled down to the town of Mwanza at the south end of the lake for a week in every month. This lasted for about six months when I helped out the Tanganyika Government who had run out of a dentist at the time. (Catch the lake steamer at 6pm on Saturday night and arrive at 7am on Monday morning - all very pleasant. I could write a book on the adventures of a dentist in East Africa). At the Mwanza Club they had several GP14's as their basic fleet. As a result of this I hatched a plan for the Kisumu Yacht Club, (being Sailing Secretary at the time). A friend of mine had been posted and wanted to sell his boat, I bought it and took it back to Kisumu.

As a good stable boat suitable for all ages the interest was immediate amongst a lot of members. Ignoring the moans and groans of the geriatrics, who, in every club did not want to see any change. We ordered 6 kits from England. Within a couple of months, building them all at once (production line style) with everybody helping, we soon had a nice little fleet to start with. The members increased steadily after that.

Racing increased and improved dramatically as we now had a One Class boat. I still put on an occasional race for the 'barges', to keep them happy!!! It meant that we now had a fleet of identical boats when visiting clubs came, which is essential for these occasions. Things went from strength to strength.

Interesting Diversion

Mwanza Sailing Club had an inter-club regatta with Williamson Diamond Mines (at that time one of the biggest in the world) about a couple of hundred miles south (out in the bush). Here they had a large dam as a part of the workings. The regatta was at alternative clubs in alternate years

As a trophy, Williamson presented a dagger with the hilt encrusted with diamonds and other gems. It was quite a trophy. One year it was the turn of Mwanza to go to Williamson's so they dug out the trophy which they had won the previous year, to take with them. Oh dear - one of the diamonds was missing. Much sweat and groaning to find and pay for a replacement - which they just managed to do in time. So far so good. However the story did leak out and Williamson's heard about it, no fool this boy - he revealed that all the stones were paste otherwise the trophy would have been worth hundreds of thousands of pounds. I suppose they must have felt absolute idiots for not realising this.

Diversion to other Jack Holt Boats

Jinja Sailing Club in Uganda is on the Lake at the source of the Nile. Here they had a fleet of Enterprises. Every boat had a different coloured sail - various blues, greens, reds etc. not a white sail amongst them. Made quite a sight.

About 18 months after introducing the GP14, I heard that Mombassa Yacht Club were getting rid of their Hornets (going for the 505). A friend and I bought one and this got the younger members very interested. With a bit of encouragement - I was now Commodore - we soon had a fleet of these as well as the GP's. The size of the fleet did not diminish, a lot of people had two boats and the club membership was increasing.

As we are talking of 40 to 50 years ago and independence has come to these countries, the European population has decreased there, especially in the smaller towns. I don't know whether these sailing clubs remains active.

So you see, Jack Holt was a terrific help in boosting sailing in "Darkest Africa" by producing easy to build boats to suit all types. Great fellow. Should be given a medal!

By the way

A GP appeared at the Koombana Bay Sailing Club in Bunbury about 20 - 25 years ago, brought in by a new member from Perth. It was rigged with a huge genoa and a trapeeze, I don't know if this is standard with Perth GP's. I was not impressed, some Australians will do anything to ruin a One Class boat with their desire to make the boat go faster.

Editor's Note: Jim will be pleased that we have heard that there are still GP's at the club and races take place with a club in Uganda. Also that all the GP's have Class certificates.

North American Branch

The development of Branches of the Association was always due to the initiative of one or more individuals. This was clearly demonstrated in North America, where - in 1956 - John Brooke and 6 others imported boats to Deep River in Ontario, Canada. By 1959, he had become Chairman of a North American Branch (they clearly had ambitions!) and Bill Mitchell (an exiled Welshman) of Cornwall, Ontario was Hon. Secretary. Bill's Club (Stormont Y.C.) was founded in 1958 to use the waters of Lake St. Lawrence, as it was completed to improve the St. Lawrence waterway through to the Great Lakes.

The first North American Championship was held at Brockville in 1960 and, by the following year, 5 clubs were recorded with fleets, the largest being Deep River with 16 boats and Stormont with 17. By now, they were holding a North West Ontario Championship in addition to Canadian and North American ones. 1962 may be seen as something of a milestone, as a fleet of 15 boats is recorded at Bay Waveland Y.C. in the deep south of Mississippi. More significantly, John Wright Jr. of Stone Harbour Y.C. came to the British National Championship at Torbay and won with a race score of 3rd, 4th, and 2nd! The Class had also started to spread into the Middle Atlantic States, being New Jersey and Pennsylvania USA. By 1963, Dick Bechtel was Secretary for that Area and also for the North American Association. It is perhaps opportune to mention that Messrs Brooke, Mitchell and Bechtel were all to be made Honorary Members of the International Association in recognition of their efforts. When the Middle Atlantic Area was ready to be formed, Bill Mitchell would drive down from Canada on a Friday night, meet with the locals on Saturday and return home on the Sunday. No mean effort by car at that time. Dick Bechtel has been Hon. Treasurer of the Branch since that time, an astonishing record of service. An unlikely entrant on the scene was Kippewa for Girls, a summer holiday camp in the Maine countryside, which imported 7 boats in 1963. They are still in use today.

Progress continued to be made and, by 1965, Cooper River Y.C. could boast a fleet of 24 boats and 3 Measurers. Such was the strength of the fleet that, for the Canadian Centennial in 1967, Stormont Y.C. was holding the first World Championship of the Class at Long Sault in Ontario. With 45 boats and entries from Britain, Ireland, Australia, South Africa, Trinidad and Barbados in addition to the USA and the host country, it certainly started a new trend in the Class. It was won by Jack Hoad from Barbados in a light air battle, principally with Mike Davis of Trearddur Bay S.C.

Enthusiasm was such that, in 1971, Stormont Y.C. were to hold their own 24 Hour Race, just like the one at West Lancs. Y.C. Fleets continued to develop with another World Championship being held at Stone Harbour Y.C. in 1975 with a large number of boats from the host country. Irishmen, Bill Whisker and Jimmy McKee took the title. Fleets in Canada had started to diminish but Cooper River had increased to 105 boats. Clearly the axis had moved south and was vigorous enough to welcome the 'Worlds' back in 1983 at the Corinthian Y.C. of Cape May, with a great turnout of 74 boats and a finish that was determined between 3 boats on the final beat of the last race! The Championship returned to this venue in 1991. With the Class now on the wane in the Branch, activity now revolves primarily around Cooper River, while boats turn up in many other corners of the USA.

History of the GP14 Class in Southern Africa

The first GP14 No. 3294 called 'Sunion', was built from plans by D. Mitchell, a professional ski boat builder during 1959 for Dan and Anne Van Wely of Johannesburg.

Soon after, Bill Donnelly, Dale Wright, Phillip Castell, Harold Taylor, amongst others, all built wooden GPs from plans and sailed them at East Rand Yacht Club, in Boksburg where the Class started to flourish. At a regatta held at Boskop Yacht Club an inaugural meeting of all GP14 sailors was called on March 4th 1962, to establish a committee, which would select a name for the Southern Africa branch and draft a constitution for ratification and acceptance by the parent UK Association. A month later, the first committee meeting was held at Bill and Helen Donnelley's home consisting of:

Bill Donnelly (Chairman)	Sail No. 5051 'Gay Cindy'
Dan Van Wely (Vice Chairman)	Sail No. 3294 'Sunion'
Dr. Paul Mulder (Secretary)	Sail No. 4789 'See Duif'
Harold Taylor (Member)	Sail No. 4543 'Spartus'
Dale Wright (Member)	Sail No. 4612 'Hermit'

These were the founding members of the South African GP14 Association and through their hard work and enthusiasm the Class grew in leaps and bounds. Soon, numerous boats had been built countrywide, with GPs in Durban and Cape Town. The South African Yacht Racing Association agreed in principle to register the Class with provisos that first,

an Owners' Association be established with a minimum of 12 boats on the register and that active participation at National regattas would then favour National recognition. At every regatta, people were cajoled into participating, so ensuring widespread exposure. The genoa foresail was developed and tested locally. Pressure was put on the UK Association to accept this as an alternative foresail, which took some time before being authorised worldwide.

The first AGM was held on 24th March 1963 at Donnelley's home, whereupon the following items were noted:

22 boats had been registered with the SAYRA.

40 GPs were either sailing in South Africa or under construction.

The first Round the Island Race had been sailed from LDYC earlier in the year, with the GPs putting up a very creditable performance.

The SAYRA had granted recognition as a Class, but not at national level.

Roller reefing gear for foresails, while at anchor, or sailing under spinnaker was in use.

Jib tensioning devices were being designed and approved.

A raised sheet-horse above the tiller and built in buoyancy were under review.

The UK Association sent us an antique punch bowl as a trophy to be presented at a National Championship regatta.

Bill Donnelly competes in the British Nationals held at Llandudno during the latter half of 1963.

The first South African Nationals are sailed at Saldanah during December 1963.

Bell Woodworking kits imported from the UK proved popular and a number of new boats appear in the course of the 64/65 season. Total number of boats now registered is 43.

The second National Championships are sailed at Allemanskraai dam (1964).

At the third AGM held on 12th February 1965 at the Wanderers Club it was reported that 98% of all boat owners had, by postal ballot, agreed to adopt the genoa as an alternative foresail. The committee was asked to look into the making of aluminium masts and booms locally as well as a mould for fibre glass boats.

The fourth South African National Championships were sailed at East Rand Yacht Club over Easter weekend (1966). This was to be the first of many successful regattas sailed at this venue, which was regarded as the home of the GPs in South Africa. Bill Donnelly and Mitch Mitchell were appointed as official Class Measurers by the South African Yacht Racing Assocation with all boats then being issued with local measurement certificates.

Jonathan Harrison on the left, Jonathan Sinclair on the right, preparing to race at Durban

GPs were displayed for the first time at the Daily Mail Outdoor Show where a lot of interest was received from the public. G. Lezard imported 'Slipper', 7021, from the UK and proudly displayed this brand new fibreglass hull with wooden deck to all members at the traditional 'Round the Island' party.

For the next few years, people came and went, more and more hulls were imported from Bourne Plastics in the UK., metal spars were developed locally and fleets grew and spread steadily under the enthusiastic guidance of the executive committee. National Championships continued to be held at ERYC over Easter. Relationships with the parent association deteriorated for no apparent reason, no doubt due to the general disfavour in which South Africa was held as the result of political conditions.

During 1969 the Mk2 fibreglass boat was launched in the UK and plans were made to import hulls to South Africa. At this time a new mast cost R60. While the prices of sails were pegged at R51 for a main, R30 each for a genoa and spinnaker. A new hull, fully imported, cost approximately R600 . Peter Hawkins continued to serve as Chairman, ably assisted by stalwarts such as George Lezard and Mitch Mitchell, who along with Bill Donnelly, were all thanked for their years of service, by being bestowed Honorary Life Membership of the Class. I believe that a Class is only as good as its members and the GPs were fortunate to have people such as Bill Heslop, Pieter De Nmeef, Norman Edwards, Leo Horn, and Gordon Prahm, among others to serve on the committee.

In 1970 the SAYRA took over the administration of the Class as far as accounts and secretarial functions were concerned. Local boat builder, the same Dave Mitchell who built the first wooden GP, was commissioned to make moulds for fibreglass production. This took almost a year before an acceptable hull was made. However, with new boats being readily available, fleets around the country began to grow. There were two keen sailors in Phalaborwa who sailed regularly among hippos and crocodiles on the local dam. National regattas attracted up to 20 entries with fierce but friendly competition at all levels.

After seven years as Chairman, Peter Hawkins retired, along with many of the old guard, so it was left to the younger generation to carry on running the affairs of the Association. Tim Brown, Patrick Mitchell, Gavin Horn, all grew up sailing with their fathers and became top class yachtsmen. Both Gavin and Patrick have competed in major UK and World Championship events from as early as 1980 when they were awarded sponsorship from the Jack Austin Memorial Fund.

It was during the 1980's that sailing peaked in South Africa and fleets grew countrywide. Under the guidance of Jenvey Nissen the Cape fleet increased to 20 boats. National Championships had over 35 entries, with almost 40 boats being registered at ERYC alone. At a boat show in 1984, five new boats were sold and there were no second hand boats available.

By 1990, these glory days were over and many boats lay idle. It took people who really loved sailing, such as Ken Bennetts and Richard Parker to revive the spirit. Once again through boat shows, new boats, attendance at all local regattas and participation in overseas events, the GP is alive and still sailed competitively throughout the country. Jenvey, being retired in the Eastern Cape, has built up a sizeable fleet at George Lakes Y.C. He, Ken and Richard are all worthy recipients of Honorary Life Membership, and I am proud to include myself in their company.

The highlight of the GP history in South Africa must be the 2000 World Championship event held in Durban, where we were able to see really beautiful boats from the UK and how well they can be sailed. This has inspired our next generation of sailors to continue promoting and developing the Class into the new millennium.

E. Howard-Davies

President 1954 - 1958   Secretary 1958 - 1969

Howard-Davies was known to all as Howard - He was a co.founder of our Association and probably it was through his initiative in those early years that the Class succeeded as it did.

Born in the Rhonnda in 1917, his family moved to New Quay shortly after. Howard soon became fascinated by boats and would use anything that could be improvised as a sail, rather than use oars, be it school blazer or reputedly, a cousin's skirt.

At 17 he was a cadet at HMS Conway, then joining the Blue Funnel Line in 1936 serving at sea until 1947. Ashore, he became the seamanship instructor at the Aberdovey Outward Bound School and naturally was involved with the formation of The Dovey Sailing Club.

Elsewhere you will read of the adoption of the GP and the part Howard played in this. Elected first as Chairman and then the first President of the Class Association.

When he became President, the Class was about 800 strong, as retiring Secretary there were 8000 GP's around the world. He was also a very fine helmsman, twice winning the National Championship. He was a man very hard to beat whether on sea or lake. Usually he would take one of the young cadets from the Outward Bound School or later, when he moved to Anglesey, from HMS Conway as a crew. Some of those cadets remember him well and at least one still sails a GP14 today. Latterly, Howard confined his GP sailing to the Menai Straits where his knowledge of the currents was second to none. I well remember finishing a poor second to him. By the time I came ashore Howard had packed his boat and was on the way home. If it hadn't been the 'through race' from Beaumaris to Caernarfon, we might have thought he had skipped a lap.

Howard continued to support the Association for many years after most would have found other interests. A stubborn supporter of the one design principles, he would, when convinced of the benefits, enthusiastically promote a change which enhanced the GP. He took time to support the genoa and I do not remember him sailing with one, he had had to transfer to a Fife by then to relieve the strain on his back. Howard was however converted to the Series II concept very quickly, and would have been very delighted with the wood version.

After a few years abroad, Howard returned to the UK and back on the Committee became a member adding valuable debate and experienced support. Belonging to the Lee on the Solent Sailing Club, he guided them to a National Championship which sadly he did not live to see.

No tribute to Howard would be complete without a few words about Gwen. She ran the Association Office for many years in Llanfair P.G. whilst Howard was working. She is now frail but maintains an interest in the Class and old friends in it.

Also there is Helen who supported Howard through his illness. She will be remembered by those who were at the 1988 National Championship as an enthusiastic worker for both Class and club.

Peter Sandbach

Ieuan Banner-Mendus

President 1958 - 1959

The GP Fourteen and Bassenthwaite SC

Ieuan Banner-Mendus was a founder member of the GP14 Association and was elected President in 1958, the year he won the Class National Championship at Plymouth and the year in which he was elected Mayor of Workington, Cumbria, the town in which he lived and worked as a lawyer.

Tragically he was unable to complete either of these terms of office, dying from a heart attack whilst sailing his GP, 'Lawless', in a club race on Bassenthwaite Lake in September of that year.

Shortly before his death he compiled a journal of a season's dinghy racing which he had hoped to have had published. It described races at his own club at Bassenthwaite, of which he was founder-Secretary in 1951, and the many Open Meetings which he and his wife Val, who was his regular crew, attended all over the country.

The early chapters described his switch from rock climbing to dinghy sailing, the latter sport being more compatible with bringing up a young family, and the search for a suitable boat.

Ieuan Banner-Mendus in No. 187 'Lawless' at Nationals 1955, Southampton Water

The National Champion 1957 - Mr & Mrs Richard Atkinson sailing 'Greylag' on Lake Bassenthwaite

He wrote: "In the autumn (of 1951) my wife and I visited the South Bank Exhibition, introduced ourselves to the boat section there, explained our ignorance and asked advice. We were recommended to the Yachting World General Purpose 14' Sailing Dinghy, newly designed by Jack Holt, designer of the enormously successful Cadet. It seemed just what we wanted; not too dear, hull £115, sails £17.10.0 and the original specification of the Yachting World in commissioning the design had stipulated for a stable boat able to carry four adults, with a good racing performance. Built of marine bonded plywood with a hard chine, drawing only 7" of water or 3' with the centreboard right down, this boat in the course of a few years has leapt into popularity for both inland and sea sailing and as I write, over 750 of them have been registered with the Class Association. Commonly known as the 'GP', the name is deplorably prosaic and it is a pity no inspired midwife was standing by at its birth to give it a brilliantly imaginative name such as was given to the Firefly Class. But GP it is and will, I have no doubt remain. Back in Cumberland we reported on what we had been told and then we learned the Royal Windermere Yacht Club, encouraging the development of a dinghy section, had a number of newly-designed 14 footers so we arranged to go and inspect them. The demonstrator was C.H.D.Acland, soon to become a close friend and next year to be the first GP Champion with his aptly named boat 'Pointer'. Sure enough the new Windermere boats proved to be GP's and having sailed in 'Pointer' we returned convinced she was the boat for us, and aware also of the advantages of us using the same boat as Windermere."

The GP14 was ordered from Bell's Woodworking and No.187, 'Lawless', was soon afloat and competing in the races of the newly formed sailing club on Bassenthwaite Lake. Ieuan and his wife competed outside their club and had their first major success coming second in the 1955 National Championships on the Hamble. They entered all the National Championships from the first one at Ellesmere in 1952 until 1958 at Plymouth, the year he died.

In the meantime Bassenthwaite had already produced a National Champion in 1957 when Richard and Mary Atkinson won in 'Greylag'. Many of its sailors have since won honours in the Class and one of the best remembered is Erie Twiname who, despite dying tragically young, achieved through his skill at the helm and with his pen in writing books on sailing, international respect.

Cubby Acland OBE

President 1959 - 1962

Cubby represented The Royal Windermere Yacht Club when it was one of the first three participating clubs responsible for the founding of the GP14 Class Association. He owned 'Pointer' No.31 in which he was to win our first National Championship.

A member of the committee from outset, he became President in 1959, serving for three years. During that period he earned the respect and affection, not only of the officers and committee members who served under him, but every member with whom he came into contact.

During his time as President he guided the Class through difficult decisions. The use of spinnakers and the introduction of the genoa were both contentious issues, threatening to split the Class. In the Class, now having several thousand members, strong views were being expressed with a big lobby against change. Cubby with great diplomacy and loyalty to his committee ensured that the interests of the majority prevailed.

It was their love for Cubby that inspired the committee to introduce the token gift to retiring Presidents, the Gold Badge, for service and dedication, something for which there could be no adequate reward.

All part of the fun

Jack Austin

President 1962 - 1965

J ack came to the Presidency of the Class after serving as Secretary for four years and running the Fleet Insurance Scheme. Little seems to be known about Jack's sailing prowess but there is no doubt that he understood the GP14. His knowledge of details of the boat and its construction was as good as anyone's. He was second to none in his determination to preserve the 'One Design' concept. That is to uphold the Rules as they applied at the time, with conformity to the plans to be strictly applied.

In committee he demanded that protocol be observed. Should a sub-committee member fail to support a decision of that committee he would swiftly be reminded of his obligations. However, committee business was brisk and enjoyable. Working with Jack was satisfying, he was quick to see experience and would hand over the lead willingly, wishing only to understand each step. A late night measuring the plug for the first Bourne Plastic moulds comes to mind.

1962 National Championships

Living in Devon after his retirement allowed Jack more time for the sea. He had a motor cruiser on the River Dart, a seaworthy craft in which he made sorties at least as far as Plymouth. With this as 'Mother' boat he led some of the first GP14 Class Cruising Weeks, both on the river Dart and in Plymouth Sound.

His great contribution to the Class was the inauguration of the Fleet Insurance Scheme, you may read of this in more detail elsewhere.

Jack was both businesslike and enjoyable to work with. A much respected President.

Ken Dunlop

President 1965 - 1968

Ken Dunlop played a significant part in the early development of the Class, first in his native Ireland in the '50s, and later as Vice President of the Association before being elected President in 1965. He was a member of Holywood Y.C. on the shores of Belfast Lough, and this small, tidal club was in at the birth of the Northern Ireland Branch of the GP Fourteen Association. Ken was one of a small group of GP owners in the Belfast Lough area who met in September 1955 to set up the branch, the first 'overseas' part of the GP family. Holywood Y.C. was also where Gerry Duffin, father of Alistair Duffin, first tried his hand at building GPs.

Ken became the second Chairman of the Northern Ireland Association in 1959 and his enthusiastic and outgoing manner enabled him to play a vital role in the encouragement of new people into dinghy sailing. Recognising his leadership qualities Howard Davies invited him to stand for election as a Vice President representing the Northern Ireland Branch in 1960.

In 1962 his employment with Burmah Castrol saw him move to Glasgow to manage the Scotland and Northern Ireland Region. This enabled him to maintain his interest in GPs as a Vice President, no longer specially representing the Northern Ireland Branch, but in a more general role. This period in the early '60s saw the rapid growth of the Class and lots of technical developments were taking place.

With his sales background and engineering understanding this suited Ken Dunlop down to the ground, and he was much involved in the development of the first hull in glass fibre construction. In 1965 Ken became President and led the dramatic modernisation of the Class in 1966 by licencing the first GRP manufacturer as well as the introduction of metal spars and the new genoa.

Ken never lost sight of his roots in Ireland and played an influential part in encouraging the Association to go to Ballyholme Y.C. for the National Championship in 1969. This was undoubtably an appropriate response to the tremendous enthusiasm and support shown by the Irish in attending the Championship throughout the '60s.

On retirement in the late '70s the family moved back to live in Northern Ireland at Ballyholme, and while he had not sailed GPs for some years, he maintained a lively interest in the progress of the Association.

Following his term as President from 1965-68, Ken was invited in 1971 to become a Trustee of the Association, in which capacity he acted until his death in 1998.

Eddie Ramsden MBE

President 1976 - 1979

In 1976 we celebrated the Silver Jubilee of the GP Fourteen Class Association and it was that same year that I was elected President of the Association at Mumbles Yacht Club, during the course of the British National Championship. In those days, it was quite usual to have the immortal song "Why was he born so beautiful...", although not entirely complimentary tribute to indicate the popularity of an incoming President. It was with surprise and a sense of belonging that I received "the treatment" from the entire GP fleet during the prize giving at the end of the Championship week. I felt I had arrived! Little did I think at the time that four years later my family and I would move house to Swansea and that I should become a member and eventually Commodore of that same Mumbles Yacht Club!

I was fortunate in my term as President to have Roy McCaig as Secretary and Paul Rowan, Phil Alexandre and David Rowlands as Vice Presidents. All had enormous talents, had commitment to the cause of sailing and the GP14 in particular and most importantly, were all close and loyal friends. Sadly, neither Roy, nor Phil are with us any longer, but Paul and David have remained trusted friends throughout all of the succeeding years.

I was also fortunate in my Presidency to be host at some superb Championships. Three British Nationals, at Troon (139 entries), Thorpe Bay (134 entries) and Llandudno (123 entries) as well as two World Championships, one in Dublin and the other in Perth, Western Australia. Looking at the lists of entries from those days there are memorable names. Those who have moved on to greater things in the world of sailing; those whose children (and now grandchildren!) are emerging today at the highest level in the sport; those who have disappeared and have not been heard of for years and a surprisingly large number who have remained loyal to GP14 sailing throughout the succeeding twenty-four years.

We had around four and a half thousand members in those days and twelve thousand boats had been registered in that first 25 years. It was, of course, a time when South Africa was ostracised by the rest of the civilised world, making communications with our GP friends in that country very difficult. However, on a positive note there was the welcome addition of the Finnish GP Fourteen Branch Association and the Indian Branch, although the latter never did get itself established, despite protracted and complicated correspondence about the proposed constitution.

There were also problems! On the technical front, this was the era of ultra-light construction, with retrospective withdrawal of certificates for underweight boats, and there were the rumbling consequences arising from the "Knight & Pink" affair. Following checks at the 1975 Nationals at Llandudno, certificates had been withdrawn from some fourteen boats, professionally constructed by a boat-builder on the south coast.

Economic reconstruction of the boats to enable them to measure was almost impossible, resulting in threats and counter threats of legal action between individual boat-owners, the builders and the GP Association and a resultant wholesale rethink of our rules and measurement systems.

In retrospect, the amount of work carried out on a voluntary basis to safeguard the Association and the integrity of the one-design concept was more than impressive and despite sometimes intense pressure, the Association held firm. Sadly, some notable members were inadvertently hurt by this turmoil and dropped out of sailing altogether. Twenty five years on, and the basis of the measurement system devised at the time, with the help of Ken Kershaw of the RYA to deal with the problems, is still in place, albeit in much modified form. Interestingly, it was that same Ken Kershaw that at the 1999 ISAF Conference came up with the concept of a "Classic" Class, to enable the GP14s adoption as an International Class, thus regularising the 2000 World Championship. GPs do have friends in high places!

My period as President also saw the loss of two famous past Presidents. Cubby Acland, our first National Champion and a redoubtable defender of the Lake District environment, died after a long and difficult illness. An even more severe loss was the sudden death of Jack Austin after a routine hospital operation. His role as Secretary, then President, followed by years of constant support and effort had a profound influence, not only on the development of the GP Fourteen Class, but also on the sport of sailing itself. As Howard-Davies wrote at the time, "Should the history of the Association ever be written, Jack's contribution will be unsurpassed by any of us - he gave of his time as few men would."

I was a great believer that the officers of the Association should be seen by the members "to get their backsides wet", a view shared at that time by all of the officers. As a result, I trailed my boat to as many events as I could, visiting every area in the UK at least once, although I remember being chided by, I think Paul Amos, when I arrived late at the start line of the first race of the North Wales and Wirral Championship at Aberdovey. The fleet had been subject to several general recalls and Paul quipped as I sailed up to the line, "I suppose we can get started now the b****** President has arrived!"

On the social front, I presided over the 25th Anniversary dinner and dance, as well as being host at the National and International social functions during various Championships. As President I was occasionally invited to "sing for my supper" as guest of honour at one GP14 club or another. I recall, in particular, attending the annual dinner of Nantwich and Border Counties Sailing Club, where I was royally entertained by, amongst other people, George Mainwaring and a certain Peter Sandbach! On another occasion I was at the end of season supper of Bala Sailing Club, where I recall hearing silly songs from a young(er) Martin (Toby) Taylor, who I recollect was a GP14 fleet measurer at that club.

Sailing is still a predominantly male sport, although that is changing gradually. As a result the wives of the GP Fourteen Association Officers have been as important as the officers themselves over the years. My wife Jean was an enormous supporting influence, particularly when combined with Margaret McCaig, in many ways being more effective than Roy and myself. It was a difficult balancing act at the time between sailing, work and family responsibilities and I did not always get it right. In retrospect, I realise what an enormous debt I owe to Jean for the support she gave me and her unfailing loyalty throughout.

One woman who had an enormous influence at the time was Molly Tupper, the Office Manager, whose efforts went way beyond the responsibilities for which she was paid and whose influence can still be felt in the administration of today. She came from a non sailing background and Roy McCaig and I hatched a plot to get her into a GP14, which we succeeded in doing at Windermere during the summer of 1978.

1977 to 1980 was also the period when the GP14 was the first choice boat for the Endeavour Trophy, the Champion of Champions event conducted by Royal Corinthian Yacht Club. The Class gained a lot of prestige from this association and a number of top sailors started to sail in the Class as a consequence. Commodore of the Royal Corinthian at that time was Francis Elkin. What has become a long personal friendship with him started in the most unlikely way when I rescued a certain, well-known GP14 sailor from an enraged and inebriated 6'3" Australian, armed with a bottle. Francis felt that I had saved the club and the event from embarrassing publicity and had demonstrated just the qualities needed to serve the RYA, but that is quite another story!

Francis was but one of the many chums I gained from the GP Fourteen Association and the Presidency in particular. Apart from all the wonderful friends in Britain, there is Geoff Miller, past Australian President that we speak to by phone every Christmas Day, Mike and Mary Igglesden who we stayed with in Australia in 1999 and Warren and Jean Elliott. Warren designed a "simplified" GP14 in 1979 after a heated discussion with Paul Rowan and myself over the practicality of doing so. But it turned out to be a different shape and Warren gave it a modified rig to suit trapezing by the crew. He named it the "'45" and for a few years it was the fastest growing dinghy class in Australia, with rules and constitution based upon the GP14!

I feel particularly priveliged to have been President of the GP Fourteen Class Association when it was almost at the zenith of success and influence. I gained great pleasure and pride from those three years, but the real gain has been the lifelong friendships I have made and the opening out into the whole world of sailing, which could not have been achieved without this General Purpose Boat that Group Captain 'Teddy' Haylock envisaged in 1948.

At the end of the Association Silver Jubilee Year I asked the question, "What of the next 25 years?" I shall be 87 years old in 2025 and look forward to an answer to that question at that time!

Eddie Ramsden

Paul Rowan
President 1979 - 1982

In 1979 Paul Rowan followed Ken Dunlop to become the second President of the Association from Ireland. From early in his sailing career he has been immersed in GPs, having grown up in that hotbed of GP sailing at East Antrim Boat Club in Larne Lough. Over the years he has sailed in the company of John McWilliam, 1968 National Champion and later to found McWilliam Sailmakers, Irish Olympic Finn competitor Curly Morris, and Mark Fekkes, World Champion in 1991, among other very competent dinghy sailors.

Learning his basic skills in the mid 1950s in the pre-World War II Larne Lough Sharpie Class, 12 feet long single-handers with metal centreplates, Paul honed up his wind, tide and boat to boat tactics as a member of Davy Marcus' 18 foot Highland Class crew. Around 1957 John McWilliam built GP1314 and this became Paul's first experience of GPs. In the year he left school, Paul acquired GP605 which was to be the first of 8 GPs he has owned.

In those early days, GPs were sailed, predominantly, in Belfast, Larne and Strangford Loughs, and the first Chairman of the newly created Northern Ireland Branch of the Association was Graham Chambers, a member of Quoile YC. The Chambers family built several GPs to cater for the needs of their three boys, and it was when Paul was sailing with his sister Anne, that Fraser Chambers met her, and they were to marry in 1982.

In 1969 Paul had GP8351 built by Trevor Stewart, a renowned builder of Scorpion dinghies. Modelled on the famous 'Trostan' (GP7442) built by Michael Hill, its excessively rounded foredeck and sharply pointed stem, on which the plans had no dimensions, caused great anguish at Committee. Paul was summoned to a hearing in Crewe chaired by the President, Jim Stables who was a solicitor, and was told his GP's stem profile was out of Class and should be corrected.

Meanwhile, with his accountancy training going full steam ahead, Paul had become involved with the NI Branch and with the inshore committee of the then Irish Dinghy Racing Association. His frequent forays to GB from 1963 onwards to compete in the Class Championship brought him into contact with Jack Austin, Roy McCaig and others. An accomplished helm, Paul has been runner-up in the Championship 3 times between 1968 and 1973, and later, in the mid 80s was Irish Helmsman's Champion in 2 successive years.

Having been Secretary of the NI Branch from 1970-72, Roy McCaig suggested in 1973 Paul might consider taking on the role of Treasurer of the Association.

This was a task he accepted with enthusiasm and applied himself to creating a system of financial control, which was capable of being managed remotely, and which is still used by the Association to the present day. Of even greater value was Paul's recognition, in the early 1970s, that the most cost-effective way to collect subscriptions was by the then new process of direct debit. Paul persuaded the Class to offer members a direct debit facility which, over the years, has played a valuable part in keeping membership numbers up, and costs down.

In 1979, Paul was given the honour of being elected President of the Association following his old friend Eddie Ramsden. As his presidential project, set up a working party with Nick Colbourne and David Rowlands to develop the modified old boat proposals which were intended to allow young people to rejuvenate sound old GPs for a minimum outlay. In 1991 he was invited to become a Trustee of the Association and as a partner in Price Waterhouse, his financial expertise has proved invaluable to successive Treasurers.

Paul has continued his lifelong love affair with the GP and GP people and earlier this year attended the Durban World's (his 5th) where he finished 12th overall in an event in which he says he sailed his GP13429 competently, but without flair. He is talking to Alistair Duffin about getting a wood 'Series III'! Some people are never satisfied, even after more than 40 years competing in the Class!

David Rowlands
President 1983 - 1985

GP sailing has always been about people and it is principally the recollections of people which stand out when remembering my years as President.

Maggie & I started GP sailing 27 years ago. Moving to work in Swansea we joined Mumbles Yacht Club and bought 1574 "Wufaloo" from Colin Lyons at Barry. I joined the GP committee as South Wales rep in 1976 and we had several open meeting seasons with minor successes and much fun.

Moving to Sheffield (where the water is not salty and comes in small patches) in 1979 with a new boat and two young babies started a long association with S.Yorkshire SC and a deepening involvement with Association administration. I worked as Technical Chairman for three years followed by three years as President and two as Treasurer.

We were very lucky then, as now, to have a team of keen and talented people working on the committees. Membership was higher than it is now and the travelling habit, with a week's holiday booked for the Nationals was a regular for large numbers.

Technically the early eighties saw the widening of the mast franchise from just IYE to include Proctors and Superspars. Apart from the introduction of some common sense fittings the rules committee were generally re-active to the schemes of members pushing the rules to make the boats go faster or work better. There has always been a lobby for a lighter GP but, with hindsight, the rule we should have tackled and never did, is a rule on weight distribution.

This period also covered the regular changes to licensed moulders for plastic hulls. Making money by making boats has never been easy and the dealings between the members' association and the trade have, I believe, served the members well and maintained a good supply of hulls, spars, sails and fittings.

Big efforts were made to share information and sailing experience and it was at this time when the first Basic Boating Book was published, a winter season of technical seminars held around the country with the talents of Jack Holt, Eddie Owen, Tony Lockett, Barry Richards and many others as speakers. The first rigging and sailing videos were filmed at Buxton and Hollingworth. David Smith produced/directed these, even enlisting the help of a passing hot air balloon in the Peak District to assist with aerial shots.

The annual Championships are always fondly remembered, Nationals at Holyhead and Troon; Worlds at Cape May and Mumbles.

> at Troon the McKerrigans cooking breakfast for the caravan village every morning and then running the racing; the Marsden brothers winning their first Championship.

at Cape May Ian Southworth and Richard Estaugh jointly winning the Worlds, the US Coastguard clearing the ocean of other boats for our racing and the overwhelming hospitality

at Mumbles the shear weight of numbers - a 195 boat event, Simon Relph's sailing skills, the reception attended by Molly Tupper, Jack Holt, Beecher Moore, Howard Davies and many others from over 30 years of sailing and Association history.

Mumbles 85 represented another first for the Association - an Extraordinary meeting of the members to question the Committee's decision on a floorboard rule. It was a rainy Sunday morning and we hired Swansea University's main refectory for the 200 plus members to watch the spectacle of Technical Chairman Fred Howarth explaining, and eventually convincing, the assembly of the merits of a rule change.

Roy McCaig retired as Secretary in 1985 in a handover to Peter Sandbach after 13 years. I was very pleased to have found someone in Peter to whom Roy was happy to hand over the reigns.

During the next two years a small Association technical group worked with Paul Amos on the development and launch of the double-bottomed GRP hull. John Atkinson, Nick Colbourne and I then formed a development group on a box structure wooden hull, removing the hardwood frames and duplicating the double floor system. Through models, test hulls and sailing prototypes this new construction was adopted. The Class now has competitive GRP hulls and wooden hulls which are dryer and safer to sail.

The Association's main job is to promote the sport of sailing through maintaining the boat, the programme of events for all members, the training and racing and the camaraderie. It has been a pleasure to be associated with such a successful organisation.

Graham Knox

President 1985 - 1988

Although his Presidency might have been expected by many, Graham Knox was reluctant to accept the role. He had joined the Committee in 1976 to become the Hon. Treasurer and not having served in any other way, felt unprepared to tackle some of the issues that were around.

Graham had entered the sport later than many of his colleagues at the time. While model yachting had been an occasional pastime of his father, Graham had shown scant interest in sport through his schooldays. Having joined Barclays Bank in 1958, he was selected to attend the Outward Bound Sea School in Aberdovey in October 1959. This introduction to water borne activity had some appeal and in the following spring, a family friend - who was a founder member of Hollingworth Lake S.C. near Rochdale, encouraged him to "Come along and give sailing a try". From then onwards sailing became his principal recreation. Around this time several other new members decided to buy GP14's and Graham soon joined them as a willing crew. When in 1964, one of the members died, he had the opportunity to purchase his first boat (No.285). He has stayed with the Class ever since.

Attendance at Open Meetings (he was an early participant in the Northern Bell Series) brought him into contact with many distinguished members in the north west. Good results were gradually achieved and in 1969 his first National's was that at Ballyholme in Northern Ireland. In the same year, he led his club team to an unlikely victory in the National Team Racing Championships at Bassenthwaite, sailed in appalling windy conditions, where the runners-up, West Kirby SC, suffered two bent masts and a broken rudder in the final !!

It was Eddie Ramsden's election to the Presidency that encouraged Graham to offer his services on the Committee. A year later, Jack Austen died and someone was needed to mastermind the Fleet Insurance Scheme. As "Graham knew about money" in the eyes of his colleagues, they persuaded him to take on that role. In 1981 he was also elected a Vice-President and relinquished the Treasurer's duties a year later.

In 1983 Graham demonstrated his boat handling skills for a training video that sold well for many years and was regarded as 'a first' amongst Class Associations.

Around this time it became more difficult to find volunteers for Committee tasks and in 1984 there were two Vice Presidents to choose from to succeed David Rowlands as President. One had to tell the nominating group that his work situation precluded him from continuing and that left Graham who felt unequal to the task ahead. This may be better understood when it is realised that there had been a conflict of a technical nature in the preceding couple of years. This primarily revolved around the control of the boat's weight. Paul Rowan for the T & R Committee, had proposed a corrector rule back in 1978 which had failed for various reasons. The outcome of that was that fittings and extra strengthening pieces of wood were used to 'correct' the boat's weight to the minimum permitted. Judicious positioning might possibly give some advantage. A group of members in the north west, fed up with the way this was being handled sought an EGM. Their proposal was narrowly defeated but the die was cast and Graham recognised that, somehow, a corrector rule had to be brought in. That this was achieved without further challenge was one of the successes of Graham's era. Another success was the initiation of a project that led to the creation of the Series II wooden boat. Paul Amos had come to the Committee in 1984 with a proposal for a new plastic boat

with a double bottom - so that it should be self-draining after a capsize. The Committee did not at the time necessarily recognise how far-reaching this would prove to be. After the launch of this boat the Committee turned its attention to how the wooden boat might be modified to adopt the principles learned from the plastic boat. It was Graham's task to establish a special Sub-Committee and to give them a brief which incidentally included a reference to the application of the technique to older boats, in due course.

The death of Howard-Davies in 1988, the same year as his club (Lee-on-the-Solent SC.) was to host the National Championship was a particularly sad moment. Howard had greatly supported Graham during his term as President.

Overall, it was a term that saw the Class set fair for the difficult years that lay ahead and Graham had achieved a sense of purpose.

Fred Howarth

President 1988 - 1991

Fred's Presidency started with an election battle at the AGM. When he died in 1996, after a long illness, a colleague wrote of his enthusiasm for sailing in a GP14, a sport that he had taken up later in life than most.

He had been born in Chorley in 1922 and took up an apprenticeship at Horwich railway workshops. This led to a life of engineering, work study and business consultancy. The latter particularly influenced his role in Committee. He sailed in 20 National Championships, several Worlds and countless Open and Area events. He was initially a member of Midland SC, before moving to Chase SC for more open waters. He put great time and effort into his sailing and sought to compensate for missing the odd windshift by better boatspeed, arising from a technical approach. His work experience led him to be considered ideal for chairing the Technical Committee and many would remember how he crusaded against what he saw as abuse of the building tolerances.

As President, he was immensely proud of the Class and would remind all of the value of boats. His term of office saw the membership vote to accept the revised construction of the wooden boat. He had a mind for detail and ensured that all aspects were considered, despite his own single-mindedness and strong personality. He will be remembered, not only for that character, but also for his dress and presentation. Always smartly attired in a blazer, often with a red shirt and club tie, plus a red handkerchief.

Bill Haldane

President 1991 - 1994

Peter Cotgrove with Bill at Llandudno during the 1992 National Championships

Shortly after election at the July 1991 AGM in Helensburgh, I officiated at my first major event - the World Championships at Cape May, Maryland, USA. Apart from the warm humid weather, memorable moments were the hospitality of the host club; the arrival of Hurricane Bob which necessitated the arranging of all the boats in a defensive circle on the raised ground of the nearby local coastguard, and the impeccable sailing of the new Irish World Champions, Mark and Paul Fekkes.

A few weeks later saw the climax of the Association's 40th. Anniversary celebrations with a special 'Parade of Sail' prior to the start of the West Lancs. Y.C. 24hr. Race in September 1991. The parade was proudly led by Nos.2,3,7,8, and a host of other very early boats.

Following discussions with other Committee members, it became clear that there was a perceived need for a clearer sense of direction for the Class Association. Accordingly a weekend seminar was organised for 26 people at the Plas Menai Water Sports Centre, Caernarfon, in January 1992. In addition to Committee members a broader mix was achieved by inviting Past Presidents and significant figures from other areas of sailing. Full discussions involving many aspects resulted in conclusions which were drawn together in a series of Development Plans which directly affected the policies of the Association for several years to come.

In the following year the late Peter Cotgrove was elected Chairman of the Royal Yachting Association. His arrival heralded a new and closer relationship with both the RYA and other Class Associations.

These new relationships allowed the GP Association to be influential in providing the right background for the moving of the National Dinghy Exhibition, 'Sailboat', from Crystal Palace to Alexandra Palace in the winter of 1994.

Peter Cotgrove made unprecedented visits to dinghy events including the GP14 National Championships at Llandudno in August 1992.

May 1993 saw the UK Inland Championship move for the first time to N.Ireland, where a successful event was held at Lough Erne SC.

My final duties were at the World Championships at Lee-on-the-Solent S.C. in August 1994, where 138 racing boats and 20 cruising boats attended a particularly successful event. During the course of the event it became clear that the South African Branch of our Association would be making a firm bid for a future World Championship. So ended 8 years of journeying from Scotland to Crewe to attend meetings which brought me into contact with new friends, many of which I am still in touch with today.

Ralph Chadwick

President 1994 - 1997

My introduction to sailing did not happen until I reached the grand old age of 36. This was at the Staffordshire County Council-run centre at Chasewater. Teaching was my profession and for many years I took groups of children from my school for their annual weeks' sailing course at the centre. The first boat I owned was a Mirror dinghy which I built from a kit. This for the princely sum of £78 - complete!! In 1970 I joined Nantwich & Border Counties Sailing Club, then in the following year completed the shell of a Bell hull, GP 9720, all for the price of £285, complete with sails, spars and included delivery. This was before the advent of VAT.

N&BCSC was, and still is, a strong supporter of the GP14 Class. Names like George Mainwaring and Peter Sandbach, both past Secretaries of the Association, were staunch members of the club. My connection and membership of the Association in 1972, began through an introduction to measuring by another member, Bill Doorbar. He was a fine sailor, well respected throughout the Midlands, had built a few GP's, was a registered measurer and Life Member of the Association.

It was not until 1986 that I became involved directly with Committee work for the Association; firstly as Chief Measurer, later as Vice President responsible for the Technical & Rules Sub-Committee and finally as President.

Throughout my Presidency there have been many very pleasant experiences. The World Championship at Lee-on-the-Solent marked the start of that period. It had been a fabulous event with 138 competitors plus a cruising group of 20 boats. My first official function was awarding Honorary Life Membership of the Association to George Mainwaring. A landmark in the history of my club. The year proved to be a busy one which included the acceptance and publication of the plans for the Series 1 to Series 11 conversion.

Ralph and Janet at sea

The GP Class has always had its 'characters.' Some will be remembered for being extrovert in some way, many for their outstanding skills and successes in racing, whilst others will be remembered for their enthusiastic support of the Class. Amongst the latter I shall remember two people in particular. Muriel King for her total commitment to encouraging sailors at Derwent Reservoir, not just to enjoy the sport of sailing, but to do it in a GP. The second person is Eric Mawhinney. I first met Eric when I visited Ireland during their Ruby Anniversary celebrations. The Irish certainly know how to throw a party!! He was obviously very well admired within the sailing community. I believe he built GP 706, 'Ventura' which he continues to sail. Because of his outstanding service to sailing and the GP, he was awarded Honorary Life Membership.

My term of office was not without its sadder occasions. November 14th 1995 marked the end of an era for our Class, for it was on this day that Jack Holt OBE, the designer of our boat, died. A Past President, Fred Howarth, died on 19th September 1996.

The National Championships at Brixham, Plymouth and Lowestoft have their own individual memories. Perhaps the most outstanding and pleasurable experience was the World Championship in Skerries. A fabulous event, beautiful weather, plenty of wind, first class competition, about 145 boats, loads of entertainment, another great party. The start of the Championship was graced by the presence of the President of Ireland, Mary Robinson. Ambassadors from Nigeria and their official reception for the officials, meeting friends from Australia and South Africa, all went towards making the event 'special'.

Being able to represent the Association on these many occasions has been an honour. I am grateful to everyone who supported me, particularly my wife Janet, and feel proud of being able to represent such a fine Class as the GP14 throughout those three years as President. May it continue for another 50 years.

A Brief History of the GP14 Hull

The GP14, originally sponsored by the Yachting World magazine, was designed by Jack Holt in 1949 for home construction from the then comparatively new material of Marine Plywood. It was conceived as a General Purpose dinghy and, although equipped with wooden mast and boom and with cotton jib and mainsail, it was also excellent to row and had a standard conversion for fitting a small outboard motor.

Over the last 45 years, there have been many changes to the boat, most notably glass-fibre versions, metal spars and synthetic sails, but the outer hull shape and deck have remained basically unaltered throughout that time. Most boats are now equipped with a genoa and spinnaker, but these are not compulsory. All GRP boats and most modern wooden boats have buoyancy tanks built in during manufacture. Many older wooden boats have all their buoyancy in the form of inflatable bags, but in most boats the bow bag has been replaced by a large tank built into the bow section and some have a similar tank under the rear deck.

Below is some sort of guide to the variations to be found in GP14s with some indication of the date and sail number at which changes took place.

Wooden Series I Hulls

These are built to Jack Holt's original design, with a ply skin on frames, traditionally mahogany, but many other hardwoods were used. The centreboard case was made of solid mahogany and sat on top of the hog and the mast had a square heel plug which sat in a box on the hog. Floorboards were generally three narrow planks each side, but most boats now have plywood sheets up to 380 mm wide. The only regulation governing bow buoyancy tanks is that they must not come back behind frame 2 (the aft edge of the foredeck). Within that Rule, there are several variants, some quite complicated to build, but the best is probably a tank formed by a single bulkhead fitted against the deck beam about 200mm in front of frame 2. Built-in buoyancy under the rear deck is unsatisfactory as it is difficult to fit transom scuppers and the boat may therefore be difficult to manage after a capsize.

These have proved very long-lived and many boats of the first 100 built are still regularly sailed at over 40 years of age. Many of the earlier boats are amateur built and they may be better, or they may be worse, than professionally built boats. All wooden boats up to 1990 were built in this way and several more have been built since, both amateur and professional.

Weight Reduction (1983)

It seems inevitable that boats become heavier as they get older, so a group of modifications were approved with a view to enabling owners to bring older boats down to minimum weight. These include reducing the number of deck beams and seat slats, lowering the height of the washboards, replacing the original centreboard case by one constructed from 6mm ply and replacing the transom by 5mm ply.

Mast Step Conversion (1991)

The square mast step set straight onto the hog can cause problems in boats which have not been properly cared for, the heavy loading from the mast being concentrated on a very short length of the hog. To repair or forestall such problems, the old mast step may be removed and a substantial spine fitted above the hog. This is capped with a pad which also passes over frame 2 and rests on a ledge in the centreboard case. The mast must be shortened by 100mm and fitted with a tenon heel plug which sits in a track mounted on top of the pad. If done properly, this modification is very successful and can extend the life of the boat indefinitely.

Series I / Series II Conversion (1994)

A very large job, in which the centreboard case is replaced by a modern unit which passes through a slot in the hog and a new floor is fitted somewhat higher than the original floor, then sealed to give underfloor buoyancy. Because of the scale of the work involved, very few boats have so far been converted, but the task is not beyond the resources of a keen amateur and the results have been very successful.

Wooden Series II Hulls

In 1989 two prototype hulls were produced (13098/9) as a straightforward effort to modernise the interior of the GP14, while reducing the cost of construction by reducing

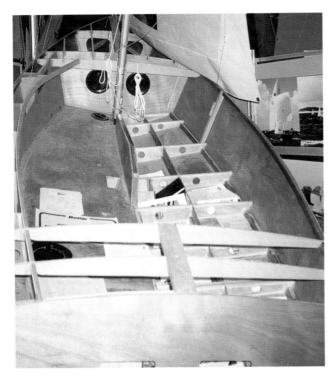

the amount of mahogany in the boat and the time required to machine frames. This experiment led to the Series II Wooden Hull, which outwardly looks unchanged, but internally has no buoyancy bags or floorboards. All required buoyancy is provided by five built-in tanks; the bow section, two small side tanks aft, and two large tanks in the space which used to be mainly under the floorboards. The centreboard case is constructed from 9mm ply and fits through the slot in the hog, giving a join which should prove to be more watertight over a longer period. As the boat floats higher in the water after capsize, the top of the centreboard case is lower than in a Series I.

Mark I GRP Hulls

First boat produced 1967, Sail No. 7002

In this original GRP version, the hulls (white) and decks (light blue) were built by Bourne Plastics at Nottingham and the boats were fitted out and marketed by a variety of firms, or even supplied as bare hulls. The hull and deck were screwed or rivetted together around bonded-in aluminium tube frames and the centreboard case capping, seats, washboards, mast step, bilge keels and rubbing beads were all wooden units screwed onto the mouldings, the floorboards also being wood. Externally, a brass keelband was fitted. Buoyancy was provided by four tanks, one each under the fore and rear decks and a short tank under the bench each side. Over 400 were produced, but the boats could be difficult to manage after a capsize and a change to the Class Rules to allow the cutting of scuppers through the transom, led quickly to the development of the Mark II Design.

The registered sail number was engraved on a metal plate glued to the hog aft of the centreboard case, but many of these plates are now missing. There should also be a separate builders plate showing a works number which may enable the Association to trace the sail number.

Several of these boats were equipped with wooden decks similar in specification to those on the Series I Wooden Hull to produce the so-called Composite Boats.

Mark II GRP Hulls

First boat produced 1969, Sail No. 7930

Externally these boats look very similar to Mark I hulls, although the bilge keels are now part of the GRP moulding. Internally, the tank under the rear deck disappeared and the side tanks were enlarged, so that they stretch from the shroud plates right through to the transom. This leaves the centre section of the transom visible from inside the boat, so that circular scuppers can be fitted, enabling the boat to be drained much more quickly after capsizes. The design proved extremely successful and many were built for educational establishments and club use, as well as for individuals. This variation was introduced by Thames Marine, but Bourne Plastics also adopted it and continued with the manufacturing and marketing arrangements as for their Mark I boats, building over 1600 hulls. Thames Marine supplied their boats fully fitted out and ready to sail and built about 260 boats with sail numbers between 8012 and 9314. About 50 hulls numbered between 10682 and 11325 were built in Northern Ireland by McComb Boats, at first using the Thames Marine moulds and later a set acquired from Bourne Plastics.

Mark III GRP Hulls

First boat produced 1977, Sail No. 11487

A further refinement of the same basic design, many of these boats are fitted with a glass-fibre mast step and include a king post to give more support to the deck around the mast slot. The decks come in a variety of colours and shades and there is no moulding for a sheet horse at the transom. The foredeck is more rounded than on the earlier boats and is patterned to give a more interesting appearance. Bourne Plastics built about 70 of these boats until, in 1978, the moulds were passed on to McNulty Boats who produced a further 50 hulls (numbers between 11695 and 12515). Approximately 80 Mark III boats were also produced by Spectrum Boats, their sail numbers ranging from 11802 to 12152.

Fibredon Mark IV FRP

First boat produced 1983, Sail No. 12516

Although buoyancy was distributed as in the Mark III boats, the Fibredon hulls marked a radical departure from previous practice, including foam, as well as glass, reinforcing. Except for the floorboards, all visible wood was eliminated from the design, so that there is no varnishing of bits here and there. The hull and deck are securely bonded together with a roll-over fibre-glass rubbing bead and the keelband is part of the moulding, except alongside the centreboard slot where separate strips are needed to hold the slot gasket. Fibredon delivered ready-to-sail boats direct to the customer and provision was made in many boats for the control lines to run under the floorboards towards the thwart. Available in a wide choice of colours, these boats proved to be very popular and about 200 were produced up to sail No. 13105.

Amos FRP Boats

First boat produced 1987, Sail No. 12800

This was the first GP14 design in which the buoyancy was provided by tanks enclosing the space under the floorboards. They retained the square mast step and had a deep well around the mast step between the bow tank and the underfloor buoyancy. About 35 boats were produced by Amos up to sail No. 13045 and 3 boats were later produced by Storrar & Relph from the moulds. Also, in 1995, Dragons produced a handful of boats with deck and hulls similar to the Amos Boats, but with full-floor buoyancy and raised mast step.

Fibredon Mark IVa FRP

First boat produced 1992, Sail No. 13120

Fibredon responded to the introduction of the Series II Wooden Hull by adding a new tray to their successful hull and deck designs, producing a boat with full underfloor buoyancy and Series II mast track, but retaining the original higher centreboard case. At sail No. 13270, a change was made to the ventilation arrangements for the hull, the floor hatches being omitted, while in 1995 a complete new set of moulds were introduced, the prototype being 13410. Production ceased in 1996 at sail No. 13492 after the building of 129 boats.

Holt-Speed FRP (& GRP)

In 1996, Speed Sails launched their all-new plastic hull, built in brand new moulds formed from patterns built by Neil Thompson. With first sail No. 13477, this design has the very clean lines typical of modern dinghies, but retains exactly the original hull shape and has a deck which is recognisably GP14. Inside, the buoyancy has been rearranged to give greater stiffness to the hull and to reduce the tendency to turn turtle. The under-floor tank is carried up to the top of the case sides and also forms the transom knee. The bow tank stops some distance below the deck, but has a large ridge which supports the centre of the foredeck. The hull, now marketed solely under the Speed name, is available in a stiff fibre-reinforced form for competitive racing and a rather more rugged glass reinforced form which appeals to sailing schools. Up to June 2000, 118 have been produced.

Current New-Build

Of the last hundred boats registered, 67 have been plastic and 33 wooden (4 home-built), giving a ratio of about 2:1. This is not unexpected, as those of our top helms who sail Speed boats, feature prominently in the prizes, alongside other top helms who prefer wood. Modern finishes on wood have dispelled the myth that you must buy plastic to cut down on maintenance and a new wooden hull reasonably cared for, can go well over five years without any maintenance beyond polishing. The availability of fine wooden boats and the opportunity for home-build, help to continue the long tradition of our Class.

If you want a plastic boat, the only one currently available is the Speed product. Current wooden builders, in order of recent productivity only, are Alistair Duffin, Derek Jolly, Tim Harper, Robson in Lakeland and Steve Boon. Kits for home-building in wood are available from FyneBoat Kits of Coniston.

The information contained in this article has been gathered from a number of sources, particularly from the New Boats Register kept by Irene at the Office. The records in this book have been compiled as numbers were issued from 1971 and are therefore original, but earlier records were filled in by Molly Tupper on the basis of her research in other documents.

Roy Nettleship

Measuring Up

THE G.P. FOURTEEN CLASS ASSOCIATION

NOTES
ON MEASURING

She looks absolutely glorious. What a joy to let your fingers run over that satin smooth skin. Such elegant curves and slender beam. As for that lovely flat bottom - what can one say? To think that I have been invited to spend the next few hours with this beauty, and at the owners' request. Measuring does have some advantages.

Gilbert, of Gilbert and Sullivan fame, wrote a line in the Pirates of Penzance, "A policeman's lot is not a happy one." Fortunately, a Measurer's lot is a far happier one when policing the rules of building a GP. When recently measuring a boat, the owner admitted that the experience of watching was quite stressful. He likened it to the stress related to waiting for the arrival of a newborn baby. A sharp intake of breath doesn't help very much either.

Throughout the history of the GP, there have been numerous changes. As things have changed, so too have the rules necessary to ensure that every boat is as much alike as possible. Some changes have developed from builder's ideas, through variations due to differing interpretations of the plans and rules, or quite deliberately to take advantage of the progress made in materials and building techniques.

Methods of measuring have been quite varied over the years. Equipment has become more sophisticated and the requirements of measuring more detailed. Through the measuring forms over the last fifty years, these developments can be traced. Compare this early example, with the present day form.

The majority of the early boats were amateur built. The tolerances gave a degree of latitude to the builder in case of errors. As professional builders came onto the scene, so too did the ability of such craftsmen to build consistently within the tolerances. Bell Woodworking was something of a household name for kits; part built hulls as well as fully fitted out boats. It has to be said that builders were, and still are, looking for the most competitive and efficient shape possible within the confines of the rules.

Measurers have a responsibility to ensure that all boats conform and in the case of any differences to report the fact to the Association. As new ideas were adopted there were often instances where advice was sought. Such changes saw the move from cotton sails to synthetic fabrics, the introduction of the genoa and spinnaker, the addition of GRP boats, metal spars, a new construction technique culminating in the current Series II boats. Regular updating of information forms an important role for the Measurer.

Flotation and measurement - Paul Amos FRP prototype.

Whilst reading some past minutes of the Technical & Rules Committee, I came across this entry which was in response to a Measurer's referral. "Following careful measurement of the sail, the T&R agreed that this sail measures in accordance with Rule 12.7(c) and advises the measurer in question that he should certify the sail, subject to the owner removing the skull and crossbones".

To a large degree, Measurers were left to their own devices on the method they adopted. When measuring the under water shape, many used straight edges across the hull and dropped plumb bobs to determine the correct measurement. Could be tricky if it was done outdoors with a breeze blowing. Similarly there was a system consisting of a wooden lattice 'frame', which was placed on the upturned hull with all the station points located by cross beams and once more, all the measurements taken by dropping plumb bobs. It was rather unwieldy and difficult to keep level and secure on the hull.

The late Bill Doorbar, a fellow club member at Nantwich, who used wooden blocks placed under the hull in its upright position, then measured the shape using the blocks to re-create the base line, first introduced me to the art. This relied upon the floor being both level and flat. Around 1984, a system using gauges was developed. Consideration was given to eliminating actual measurements by adopting "GO" and "NO GO" gauges. It didn't seem to meet with much success

One of the biggest problems for a Measurer was being able to accurately determine every station point. The most difficult was around frame 1. Because of the complex curvature of the hull at this point, the slightest inaccuracy, either fore or aft, could give a wide variance in the resulting measurement.

Jimmy McKie and Ralph Chadwick, measuring at the 1988 World Championships - Howth, Ireland

For quite some time 1 experimented with various methods of how to measure a hull both accurately and quickly. My theory was based upon using the properties of a parallelogram. A calliper was made using angle aluminium attached at right angles to a frame. The frame lay along the keel, supporting the cross beam across the hull. Four rigid drop arms were secured at right angles to the crossbeam so that they dropped vertically onto the hull. The parts were machined so that the arms could be moved both vertically and horizontally, then clamped in place.

By placing the drop arms onto the hull, then removing the whole frame from the boat, you were left with the four points of the chines/sheerline which could then be accurately measured for both depth and beam.

Through development work with John Ballinger, who was by trade an engineer, we eventually managed to create the jig which is in use to-day. It takes out any guesswork, can guarantee consistent and accurate results and saves more than an hour's work over previous methods.

In the case of GRP boats, there is a slightly different story. The plugs for the moulds are carefully measured before the mould is made. This makes some of the measurements for a Measurer, redundant. The under water shape is fixed. Periodically hulls are taken for check measurements to ensure that nothing about the moulds has altered. This practice continues to-day.

Paul Amos and Nick Colbourne

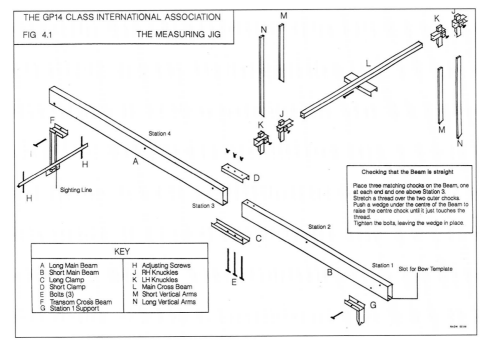

All plans for the Mast Step Conversion, the Weight Reduction Plans, the Conversion of a Series 1 boat to the specification of the Series 11, with their relevant measurement forms, are fully up to date. In 1996 Roy Nettleship re-vamped the Measurers manual, which is now a very comprehensive document, the envy of many Classes.

Ralph Chadwick. Measurer 307

Acknowledgements :-
Research by Molly Tupper, Irene Thompson, Maggy Ernshaw from documents in the Association archives, R.Nettleship for article published in the Basic Boating Book.

The Office over 50 Years

At the first meeting of owners of GP14s, held in Shrewsbury in November 1951, Mr D.Barlow was elected Hon-Secretary and held the post for the first year. Much of the work must have been coping with the new membership and setting up systems to cope with their needs and those of the Committee. In the earliest years, measurement of boats was not as rigid and detailed as it later had to become. His successor was the famous 'Dusty' Pollock, a Director of Bell Woodworking who was anxious to see this new 'child' become properly established.

Irene Thompson

By 1954, there must have become enough members, independent of the kit manufacturer, to find a volunteer to take on the increasing workload. Jack Austin, who worked for a Manchester based Insurance Company, was used to the routine of office needs and had a wife to help him and was duly elected. A year later he was to initiate the Fleet Insurance Scheme also. In holding the position until 1958 (together with the post of Hon. Treasurer), he was backed up by an enthusiastic President in the shape of E. Howard-Davies. Howard was the owner of GP No.1, having been a member of Dovey Sailing Club (as it then was) when the club adopted the Class. At the time, he was an instructor at the Outward Bound School in Aberdovey where his love of the sea could flourish. He moved to join the tutorial staff at HMS Conway and lived at Tan-y-Coed on the Menai Straits. It was now his turn to take on the role of Hon. Secretary and also double up as Hon. Treasurer. His home became the base for the Association Secretary's Office until 1969. In addition to his wife, Gwen, Howard employed additional clerical staff to help out when needed. This long period of duty (coupled with much racing success on the water) attracted the cachet of 'Mr GP14' to Howard. With a membership now around 4000 people, the Association's work began to show strains.

Maggie Earnshaw

Although re-elected Hon. Secretary of the Association at the AGM in 1969, held during the National Championship at Ballyholme Yacht Club (in Northern Ireland), Howard-Davies' fellow officers became aware of the strains in his life at that time. They cast about to find a volunteer to appoint and ease Howard to cope with other tasks. George Mainwaring, recently retired from the Post Office, agreed to volunteer his services and set up a permanent office with a view to making the role of the Secretary less involved in routine administration. They wanted to find an Office Manager who would be free of 'Committee politics' and able to deal with all routine matters unsupervised. George fortunately lived near Newcastle (Staffs.), as the Association Committee already met in the nearby Crewe area, for convenience. He made his caravan available as temporary accommodation, and to keep the Association's affairs as far out of his home as possible! Several trips were undertaken to Tan-y-Coed to collect all the records and he then set about looking for a permanent office and staff to employ. Interviews were arranged and premises inspected. Luck was on George's side as a widow, Mrs Molly Dodgson with much clerical experience, met the criteria. She was to have a helper, Margaret Blunt and they would form an excellent team, as Molly was able to take on a degree of executive responsibility. They found a convenient office too, above a shop on the Nantwich Road in Crewe and there the Association has stayed to this day at No.129b.

George had not intended to take on the role of Secretary for more than a year, but found it soon extended to three years. He had however again found how helpful Presidents could be, for Roy McCaig had taken on that role in 1970. When he wanted to step down in 1972, Roy still had another year to run and Philip Alexandre stepped into the breach. Meanwhile, misfortune had hit the McCaig family with the disappearance of their eldest son, David. Perhaps it would compensate in some way, for Roy now plunged himself fully into the running of the Association, holding the post for the next 12 years. With a sharp technical mind, an eye for detail, and a good sense of correct procedure, Roy was an ideal person for the task. Ably assisted by Molly - who had by now re-married, and become Mrs John Tupper, they formed a partnership that saw steady progress. Margaret left the Office in 1977 and Irene Thompson joined the staff, a few months before her departure. There

The office staff in 1964, preparing that year's handbook.

had been re-organisation of the Association to meet its management strategy and recognise its international dimension. The title was amended to include the word 'International' (as an Association, not the Class which even then was only granted as a status by the International Yacht Racing Union) for members outside Britain had been given local Branches. Branches were supported in Ireland, North America (ie. Canada and the USA), Australia, South Africa and Zimbabwe. Roy served four Presidents loyally. Meanwhile, Molly Tupper, now assisted in the Office by Vera Davies, began to find her health deteriorating. She too had served the Association Officers and members with loyalty and would soon need to retire.

A change of President in 1985 saw a new team in, with Peter Sandbach joining as Secretary. Peter had been a Measurer from 1960,on the Committee from 1967 to 1971 and involved in 1968-70 with the Rules revision on the Tech. Sub Committee. Peter had also represented North Wales on the RYA Council for Wales for several years up to 1972. Having spent a year looking over the shoulder of Roy and undertaking the technical correspondence for Roy, it seemed logical to take on the whole secretarial responsibility.

The transfer of the records of the Association to computer and training our staff, occupied much time and not a little gentle persuasion. It could now be said that we could not operate without the computer.

The Association voice was being heard more in RYA circles and Peter joined the Class Associations' Committee in 1988 becoming Chairman in 1990. From 1993 he was the Class Associations' elected representative on Council of the RYA., and also on Sailboat Committee.

After 7 years and helping three Presidents, Peter felt it was time to take a well-earned break. Vera Davies also decided it was time to retire. By some good luck again, Graham Knox had become free to take on the Secretary's role when, in March 1992, Barclays Bank asked him if he would consider taking early retirement! Staff interviews again were needed and Margaret O'Connor (better known now, after re-marriage as Maggie Earnshaw) passed the test and joined Irene to keep the Office running.

The pace of computerisation and technological changes have made their impact too. First steps in this field were undertaken by Past President, David Rowlands in 1984. Peter Sandbach then got himself trained up and increased the pace and extended the range of records held on file. Today, with fax, on-line working, the website and an excellent photocopier, the Office has most of the facilities demanded in such an environment.

Association Secretaries

1952 - 1953 David Barlow

David Barlow was a member of Dovey Sailing Club and became the Secretary at the first AGM. The initiative for forming our Association came from E.H.D. and David, who lived in Stourbridge, must have had a busy year keeping up with the rapid adoption of the GP by clubs round the country. Maintaining contact with clubs, Yachting World and Bell Woodworking to develop the rules and specification of the boat. At the end of that year there were 115 registered members.

1953 - 1954 Dusty Pollock

As owner of Bell Woodworking and being the builder of most of the boats at that time, Dusty had been issuing the Sail Numbers. It was on an 'allocation to club' basis at that time. Numbers being filled in as members took delivery of their boats. Dusty was an enthusiastic racing man, a boat builder and knew well both Haylock and Holt, so it was useful in this year of consolidation for the secretaryship to be in the Bell camp.

1954 - 1958 Jack Austin

Jack was a perfectionist, exact in all he did. It was he who introduced the initial registration form and the filing system still used to this day. A stickler for precision he had all measurement certificates invalidated and after revision of the rules all boats were re-measured. Much of this centred on the chine at frame No.1. Foundations were laid for sound measuring practice.

Jack, working in the insurance business, introduced the Insurance Scheme. The first Handbook was printed and at the end of 1956 over 1000 members were recorded.

By the end of 1958 there were 2600 members and nearly 2500 boats registered.

1958 - 1969 E. Howard-Davies

Howard had moved from Aberdovey to Anglesey to be on the staff of HMS Conway, the Merchant Marine Cadet Training ship. On retiring as President he took over the job of Secretary. He had plenty of accommodation at Llanfair P.G. and an office was established there which remained until he retired in 1969.

The Association was growing at a tremendous pace during this period; frequently over 100 letters would arrive per day, his wife became the Assistant Secretary.

1969 - 1972 George Mainwaring

On Howard's forced retirement to seek a teaching qualification, George, a Vice President and recently retired, took over at short notice. He moved the contents of the office to a caravan which he obtained and sited at his home near Newcastle, Staffs. Jack Austin brought his touring caravan and lived alongside for a few weeks to show George the ropes. Molly Dodgson joined the team as office manager and many of the procedures set up then are still in use today.

This temporary arrangement agreed by George lasted three years during which time the present office in Crewe was opened.

1972 - 1973 Philip Alexandre

Philip filled in for the year until Roy McCaig could take over on retiring as President. He did however see through the important transfer of the copyrights of the boat from Yachting World.

1973 - 1985 Roy McCaig

Roy in his mammoth stint of twelve years, the longest of any Secretary, established himself as the upholder of protocol and good practice. Often under great pressure due to his work requiring him to reside in many far flung corners of the country. He dealt with mail before work each day and all replies were handwritten in full and despatched to Crewe, where Molly would do the rest.

Nobody on the Committee during this time will forget Roy's affection for his Scottish ancestry. Dinner at the Crewe Arms required 'full dress' a wonderful sight in his kilt. Nor may we let pass the great support that Margaret gave to Roy.

She was always to be seen at Nationals working hard so that Roy could sail.

1985 - 1993 Peter Sandbach

Before being elected Secretary, Peter spent a year as understudy to Roy dealing with Technical questions coming to the office and the issuing of Class Certificates. At this time David Rowlands had acquired a BBC computer to help tackle the insurance business. Neither knew much about them at the time and a few sleepless nights ensued. At year two everything ran quite smoothly. The computer was put to more use including most of the content of the Handbook which has considerably held down costs.

This was a period of rapid development of Series II, and much testing was done.

The Plas Menai training week was inaugurated in 1990 in memory of Howard-Davies. Working with Bob Bond, a course was evolved which differed in as much as our own boats were used and the importance of crewing skills included. Hitherto, on sailing courses at Plas Menai, the emphasis had been on helming.

Peter was elected to represent Group B on the RYA Class Association's Committee becoming Chairman. In 1993 he was elected to represent all Associations on the Council of the RYA. He was awarded the RYA 'Yachtsman's Award' for his services in 1998.

1993 - Graham Knox

Graham came to the post as the most experienced person in the Association. Having been President and Treasurer and managed the Insurance Scheme, there was little he did not know. His wise mind and adept diplomacy has guided us through the most difficult years the sport has experienced since the rapid growth in the 50's & 60's. Not only have there been more interests which compete with sailing, but the influx of new designs have attracted the younger and a few older members away from the Class. Through all this we remain one of the strongest Class Associations in the sailing world.

The GP14 Class
Fleet Insurance Scheme

In the earliest years of the Association, the need for boat insurance may not have seemed a high priority. It was a limited and specialised market for insurance companies and it cannot have been a competitive one. However, as we shall see, the Association became a leader in this field and the continuing success of the Class Association owes much to the success of the Insurance Scheme.

As the Association rapidly expanded, one member of the Committee, Jack Austin, could see a need for insurance specific to the needs of members. Jack, then living in Stockport, worked for an insurance company and was friendly with Edmund Hine, another GP14 sailor, who worked for a major Manchester insurance broking business. Between them, they devised a plan for a special sailing dinghy insurance exclusively for GP14s. This was to be the first Class Fleet Insurance Scheme, when it was launched - for the start of the sailing season - on 1st April 1955. The renewal date was thus fixed for the years to come. It was also to be the forerunner of many other schemes set up by Edmund Hine for other Classes, but he agreed that the GP14 one should be 'Jack Austin's'. They entered into arrangements with Navigators & General Insurance to underwrite the Scheme and provide a simple and straightforward policy. This gave a considerable benefit to members and the Association from a share of the commission received.

Navigators & General had commenced business in 1921 to assist mariners who lost their Masters Certificate and to help improve mariners' rights and its policies were guaranteed by Eagle Star. In 1923, Navigators introduced the first ever specialist yacht and motor-boat insurance policy using simple, plain English documentation. The company became wholly owned by Eagle Star in 1960. It has remained the underwriter to the Fleet Insurance Scheme, proving to be an excellent choice for the relationship.

The Insurance Scheme was not without a challenge. In the late 1950s, a newly formed business started a 'Helmsman's Policy' and included the outline of a GP14 on the application form to imply that it might have been recommended by the Association. An injunction was quickly served to prevent them using this 'image' to promote their policy to members.

Steadily, the Scheme built up a reputation for good cover and service to members and, at one time, had some 4000 policy-holders. In the early years, the policy gave a standard value cover with few options. It was operated through a master policy with certificates being issued to individual members. Gradually, as the cost of new boats rose against the 'stock' of older boats, it became necessary to build in a stepped premium for sums in excess of a base. Jack Austin kept a watchful eye on claims and handled affairs with utmost aplomb. By the mid-1970s, Jack was ready for retirement and moved down near

Dartmouth. He had organised matters with Navigators so that they effectively dealt with all the administration of the Scheme and the Association simply received commission on the premium income. Then, in November 1977, Jack had to go into hospital and sadly passed away. The Association Committee had to take action, as renewal negotiations were due.

Graham Knox had been elected to the position of Hon. Treasurer at the AGM in 1977, having served a year's apprenticeship. As he worked for a Bank in the Manchester area, the Committee thought that he should be the one to take on the Scheme. Claims had been increasing and one or two members needed a sharp reminder about their claims record and there was much to learn in a short period. However, the takeover proceeded successfully and the Association continued to benefit. By the 1979/80 renewal year, the basic premium was £13 for an insured value of £550 (with a £10 excess on any claims). At the same time, the Association subscription was £3.73.

Concerned with their own rising costs and plans to reorganise their business, Navigators & General asked the Association to take over the policy records in November 1980. A 10% No-Claims was introduced in the following year, increased in 1988 and again in 1994. Next came a discount for members who did not race. In March 1985 came the major task of computerising the records. Now the basic premium had doubled to £26 for an insured value of £750 and a claims excess of £25 was set to stem a rising level of claims, with the increase in average costs of such claims. The Association subscription had also increased to £7.76 (though this sum was held for 5 years from 1983, despite inflation). During this period, Navigators had closed down all but one of their regional offices and made Brighton their headquarters. So they looked for further savings and asked Graham Knox to take over the administration of claims and handle the sanctioning of the large majority of smaller claims. That has worked well for the benefit of members generally, leading to quick settlement. But recent years have not been without problems as competition in the insurance market 'hotted-up'. The basic premium of £50 for £900 minimum value was held steady from 1996 to 1998 (the Association subscription was now £14) and new entrants in the market were offering lower premiums - although their cover was probably not as generous. So, with steadily improving claims experience, it became possible to reduce premiums for the first time to a basic £45 with a comprehensive restructuring to make the whole scheme simpler.

Overall, the Association Fleet Insurance Scheme has contributed greatly to the benefit of the Association by giving its members excellent value insurance, whilst providing a useful stream of income from the commission earned. When the Committee wanted to set up a Travel Grant Fund in Jack Austin's name, they wisely decided to fund it by taking a 10% share of the net commission received. That too has helped the international spirit of the Association. Finally, it is remarkable that, in 45 years, the Scheme has only had two people with its tiller in their hands!

Championships

The GP14 was not to be a racing boat. At least that was the intention of Group Captain Haylock. In fact he is said to have actively discouraged the formation of the Association on the grounds that its proposed rules were orientated towards racing. Most of the first owners wanted to test their sailing skills in combat, whether at Shropshire, Windermere or Aberdovey sailing clubs. How the Group Captain could have thought otherwise, we shall never know. With racing being the backbone of club activity, competition with other clubs soon followed at a local level. It seems that there may have been team racing of a sort before Open Meetings. Certainly team events took place in the North West before the first National Championship at Shropshire S.C. in 1952.

It would require another volume to this book to write about each of the 21 different venues of our National and a further 7 for World Championships The list of these is at the back of this book. I do not propose to mention each one which does not mean that the others did not have merit, they did.

One of the first decisions of the Committee was that our first Championship would be held and that it would be at Shropshire Sailing Club. The club, by a lake, Whitemere, is at Ellesmere, Shropshire, one of the most beautiful locations on the circuit. We do not have the results of that first event but from the photographs it would seem that about 30 boats entered. The lake is surrounded by trees and is noted for fluky winds. However the sailing has always provided a challenge and frequently, plenty of excitement. The National

Thorpe Bay
World Championships,
July 1971

Championship quickly became so popular that it was impractical to return to Whitemere, however they continue to hold one of the best supported Open Meetings in the calendar, always in September.

The Competition at Troon SC, Nationals 1984

It was natural that in the first years of the Association, the Championship should take place at the clubs which were the first to adopt the GP. New Quay, R.Windermere, Hamble, Holyhead, Bassenthwaite, all were hosts to the event which took place over a weekend. Naturally enough these clubs produced the Champions. You may have noticed that the founding club, Dovey Sailing Club is not included. They have hosted many Area Championships but never the Nationals. Some of their members claim that they held the first in 1951 when they had visitors from New Quay and Shropshire. Yes, they held the first GP Open Meeting but it was before the Class was formed.

In 1956/7 the Committee decided that all National Championships should in future be held on the sea. They had already been to New Quay and Holyhead, proving the seaworthiness of the boat. They also decided on a sequence of three clubs, Llandudno S.C., Thorpe Bay S.C., and R.Torbay Y.C. so distributing the event geographically. The fourth year in the sequence would bring in another club, so taking the event to all regions of the U.K.

The National Championship soon established itself as not just another sailing weekend, for at this time it changed to a full week. Competitors and their families looked for more than the five, sometimes arduous, races. This came about when the more enlightened clubs provided entertainment in the 'off-duty' evenings.

By the 1960's the Committee was not just looking for venues which were to provide good racing but also to cater for the 'menage' of both the helm and crew. Later we were to find the average people per boat was to be nearly 5.

Thorpe Bay S.C. were the first to take this aspect seriously and entertained the fleet very professionally. Others followed with great merit. Mumbles Y.C. and Lee-on-the-Solent S.C. stand out in my memory. The exceptional talents of the Ladies Committee at Mumbles has to be the highlight of all. Do you remember? The last time we went to Troon stands out in memory, perhaps that was because with very few exceptions everyone camped by the clubhouse. A 'green field site', it seemed a wonderful week-long party.

All clubs are different and it is the variety that contributes to the success of our Nationals. I do not think that any one place provides everything that everyone could wish for. Deciding which aspects are the most important often taxes the Committee to the limit. Although some years may be perceived as better than another, there is one thing all Championships have in common, everyone enjoys it and would not have missed it.

It may be strange that I have not talked of the sailing yet, after all that is what we go for. Providing for good racing does not always come easy. You meet all sorts of people with differing experience in running championships, they vary from ones who have done it all

A wild return at Lee-on-the-Solent

before and wonder why we should wish to meet, to those who invite a meeting 12 months in advance and ask "what would you like?".

As costs of organising Championships has risen over the years so have the expectations of the participants. Two people who were regularly involved with our Championships have played a major role in raising standards, not just for ourselves, but nationally and internationally. They are the late George Wilson and Tony Lockett. Together they wrote the RYA - YR4 Club Race Management book. Tony has gone on to be one of the most highly respected authorities on event management in the world.

The clubs that we have visited have provided a wide variety of experience of sailing on the sea. At least a wide open space, for the Clyde and The Solent are hardly open sea. For many this is an annual experience and the only time that they have the opportunity. Some find the tides and currents a torment even unfair, to some the mystique adds to the joys of the racing.

Our Championships have above all else brought together people who have a love of sailing the GP and the people who sail in them. Racing in a GP does not for most bring an expectation of being this year's Champion, but of doing a little better amongst the group that one inevitably finds sailing together in these races. The introduction of the Silver and Bronze Fleet competition gives that little extra edge to competition within the fleet.

The Champions

45 National and 12 World Championships have produced 32 different Champions. What do they have in common? Fine sailors all of them. A few have gone on to fame in the International Sailing World whether on the water, in the loft or any of the other talents that have something to do with boats. To many, sailing was wholly divorced from their

profession, so it seems difficult to say what makes a Champion. However having met three quarters of them, one thing they do have in common is modesty, the catalyst to their strength in determination and skills.

Whether in calm or storm, for we remember both, (Llandudno! Largs! Lee on the Solent!) Whether Acland, Allen, Owen or Estaugh, Penman, Davies or Nettleship, Colbourne or Coles and hundreds more, all have left us with great memories. The 28 different clubs have each in their own way added to that wonderful heritage that we carry forward to the next 50 years.

Llyn Brenig SC, NWT Wirral Area 1990

Peter Sandbach

Cruising in a GP14

The GP14 was designed as a general purpose boat and, amongst all its many virtues, it is ideal for cruising. To facilitate cruising some GP owners cut a hole in the rear decking or fit a box to the transom, to accommodate an outboard motor, or they have fitted rowlocks. Over the years the GP has been seen on many an estuary pottering about, beached at some convenient spot, or being rowed along some windless inlet. The GP14 is known for its general sea-worthiness and stability. It is the perfect boat for cruising.

At least two cruising weeks were held in the West Country when Jack Austin retired and went to live in Strete near to Dartmouth. Owning a seaworthy cruiser, he mothered the fleet on sorties up the Dart and the surrounding waters. Another year the fleet were in Plymouth.

The Elliott family in Swansea Bay

There have been several significant individual voyages in the early days. In 1959 a member sailed single handed from Southend to Calais and followed this in 1962 with a trip from Dover to Ostend. In 1963 others sailed round the Isle of Man, while in the next two years young members from Lee-on-the-Solent sailed to Weymouth and Dungeness respectively. A crossing from the Solent to Barfleur in 1966 shows just how ambitious these early cruisers were. Others have made crossings in the Irish Sea and a circumnavigation of the Isle of Mull. It is truly amazing what adventures have been undertaken in a GP.

Cruising as a fleet

The GP Fourteen Association has, in recent years, organised a Cruising Week to run alongside its National Championship events. I detail a few of the advantages of cruising with others in the GP Fourteen Association. For example, you get to visit places you wouldn't dream of attempting to sail to on your own. It is good fun to sail in company with others, even if you don't know anybody before you start, there is plenty of opportunity for a lunchtime chat whilst picnicking on a beach that means you soon get to know everyone, and the GP fleet are very friendly. If the receding tide leaves your boat high and dry then there are others willing to help lift it back to the water. A particular advantage of cruising in company is that we learn from watching: such as, what to do when it comes to anchoring and putting out trip lines; or discovering not to beach your boat on shingle so you don't get

The fleet sets off across Swansea Bay

Meryl Gover, Llandudno 1993

little pebbles stuck up your centreboard casing. These organised cruising weeks are accompanied by a support vessel, which is crewed by people with local knowledge who can suggest a good place to go in the prevailing conditions. An advantage of having a support vessel is that if the wind drops and the tide is against you, a short tow will often get you to the wind, and you manage to get home again in time for tea. Something particularly enjoyable about cruising alongside the Nationals is joining in with the racers at the evening social events organised by the host club. One of the biggest bonuses of cruising with the GP fleet is that it is just great fun! A lovely way to spend a holiday.

People who cruise

People who go cruising with the GP fleet may race at their home club yet don't feel the urge to compete in the bigger events. Perhaps they feel they will be in the way. Some have joined the cruising fleet to experience their first taste of sea sailing, and, having tested the waters and rubbed shoulders with racers, have progressed to racing with the main fleet at a Championship. Other intrepid souls venture on longer passages in their GP, or even camp on board. One has only to read the annals of the Dinghy Cruising Association, or the GP Fourteen Association magazine Mainsail, to learn of their adventures.

Organised GP cruising

Organised GP cruising started in 1988 when Lee-on-the-Solent Sailing Club arranged a cruising event alongside the GP14 National Championship. The Solent is a wonderful place for cruising. Our group's first sail across the Solent was to Wootton Creek on the Isle of Wight where we had lunch at the Royal Victoria Yacht Club. On Monday we sailed to Seaview, later skirting past Cowes harbour, which looks very different when viewed from the sea. On Tuesday, after calling in at Seaview for lunch, we visited the river Hamble, a distance of 15 nautical miles. The sail up river as far as Warsash was easy enough, but the return presented us with a 'very interesting' beat out in a good force three, having to negotiate a passage through all the moorings.

That first cruising week at Lee-on-the-Solent was a great success, and the idea of running a Cruising Week at the same venue as the National Championship took off. A programme of sailing during the day, then mixing with the racers in the evenings for the social events proved an ideal combination.

Time to leave Pwll Du

Cruisers at Mumbles YC 1989

In 1989 Mumbles, in South Wales, was the venue for the Nationals and Cruising Week. Our first cruising destination was a trip out past the lighthouse and on to Pwll Du cove for picnics. On Monday, sailing past the Swansea Marina along the coast towards Neath was made more interesting with the wind strength increasing enough to get a boat with four up onto a plane. Tuesday's light wind encouraged an amount of pumping, rocking and 'smooching', all quite legal and some positively encouraged in cruising. On arriving at the Civic Centre beach it was discovered that everyone had a different approach to setting the anchors. They included throwing the anchor as far as possible (without the warp attached - no names), wading up to one's neck, or even swimming out to set it in deeper water. The end result was the tide went out anyway and left most boats high and dry. After lunch the tide had gone out so far that the errant anchor was found and the boats had to be carried to the water. Later in the week the weather got too breezy for cruising, but it was exciting watching the brave go racing. The shared experiences, the recounting of all the happenings, new friendships made, the social activities, all these things add up to a successful Cruising Week and family holiday.

A welcome tow, Abersoch 1990

Abersoch was the destination in 1990. A week of mainly light to non-existent winds with plenty of hot, and I mean hot, sunny weather. These were ideal cruising conditions if you didn't want to go too far. Out past St Tudwal's Islands and the seals, to picnics and ice cream on various beaches were the order for the week. On one day the cruisers managed to sail beyond Pwllheli, whilst the racers champed at the bit on the shore as they had no race due to a lack of wind! A highlight of this holiday, apart from the good company and great social activities of course, was spotting dolphins amongst the boats.

In 1991 cruising was at Helensburgh, on the Clyde. Another week of light winds and sunny weather was enjoyed by all. Submarine bases, both American and British featured

Picnic on Pwl Du beach

in our destinations amongst the Lochs and Kyles of the area. A diversion whilst we were in Gare Loch took us to Mc. Gruers boatyard so we were able to take a look at Drum, the infamous racing boat (the one the keel fell off). On the Friday we went in convoy to Loch Lomond. We sailed from Ross Priory with a lunchtime rendezvous on the island of Inchcailloch. It was real 'Swallows and Amazons' as we left the island in a fresh breeze heading back to Ross Priory. The friendliness of the fleet, the beautiful location and the warm hospitality of Helensburgh were all excellent.

The August Bank Holiday weekend of 1991 saw the first GP cruise organised by Weir Quay Sailing Club, on the river Tamar. This has now been established as an annual event. Camping is arranged on the club site for visiting families. This bank holiday weekend usually coincides with the Navy Day at Plymouth dockyards, so when sailing is down river we pass all the warships in the dockyard crowded with visitors for Navy Day. Blacked up Marines can often be seen zooming around in rigid inflatables busily attacking various targets, or rescuing people. When sailing on the Tamar at certain states of the tide it gets quite shallow on the inside of bends, so some of the visitors have been known to encounter the infamous mud of the river. Lunch is usually sandwiches but, in true cruising style, a Weir Quay sailor usually produces a barbecue and consumables to go with it, so some enjoy hot dogs as well. These Cruising Weekends are a notable success.

Restronguet Sailing Club on the estuary of the river Fal was the 1992 venue. The racers were at Mount's Bay Sailing Club, at Marazion, near Penzance. The Fal estuary is a beautiful area for cruising. There were 20 boats, including seven families with children from toddlers to teenagers. Destinations included St Mawes, across the Carrick Roads, Pendennis Point, St Just in Roseland for a coffee and a visit to the local church. One evening we had a tour of St Michael's Mount, along with the racers. We also had a trip to Porthallow, a steep, shingle beach to the south of the Helford river, a distance of over 8 miles. There was a visit to Trelissick, a National Trust garden, then some people decided to head up river, past King Harry Ferry, to see the 'big boats' moored there.

The 1993 venue was Llandudno. Our first cruise was around the Little Orme to Rhos on Sea, where we enjoyed a picnic lunch on the quay in the sun. It was a long, breezy beat back to Llandudno in a force 5 wind. Our apologies to the racing fleet, some of whom we overtook on the way back, but our programme is heavily influenced by tides and opening times. Monday, Tuesday and Wednesday it was 'blowing old boots' so the cruising fleet enjoyed walks on the Great Orme, swimming and visiting the local hostelry. Tuesday saw the cruisers moving to Conway Marina, towing the boats round and settling them down on floating berths in the Marina. Thursday was WINDY, and Thursday is a day that some of us will remember for some time to come. The cruising fleet set of in a steady breeze from Conway Marina, with Penmaenmawr beach our destination for lunch. Beating out of

Cruisers at Llandudno 1993

Conway towards Fairway buoy in a steadily freshening breeze and a lumpy sea, all were enjoying the sail, when the mother of all squalls descended on us, resulting in a few capsizes, personal traumas etc. Our support boat called on the coastguard to check us out, but in the event they were not needed. Some of the fleet elected to beach their boats at Penmaenmawr, and one or two others dropped their mainsails to run back into Conway, but were still planing under genoa alone. After this incident we were struck by what a well found boat the GP is. Everybody was glad to see warmth and shelter back at the marina. After several mugs of hot tea and a few yarns later, we were planning Friday's sail up the river Conway.

Lee-on-the-Solent, where the Cruising Weeks started, was our 1994 destination. We had mainly fair weather and breezes that blew harder as the week progressed. We sailed to Portsmouth, to a beach that appeared, with the receding tide, just outside the harbour wall. We popped into town for coffee and ice creams. Other destinations included Bembridge on the Isle of Wight, when our return journey was a glorious eight mile spinnaker run back to Lee-on-the-Solent, and on the Friday a trip up the river Hamble, with a delightful lunch at the yacht club.

In 1995 we were at Brixham. This was a week notable for hot sun and little wind. Most of the week we made more progress with paddles than with sails. We made it across the bay to Torquay harbour where we moored in amongst the gin palaces before slipping ashore for a snack. Brixham had organised a sailing treasure hunt, but the wind ran out before the clues and we had difficulty getting to the right cove for the barbecue. Paignton beach is shingle at high tide and not to be recommended for beaching. Babbacombe, just round the headland from Torquay, was a good day's sail. As we rounded the headland on our return the bay was shrouded in a sea mist, so we sailed by compass bearings to find our way home. The cruisers were very kindly offered the hospitality of some bigger boats, with motors in case of a lack of wind, for a trip up the river Dart.

Royal Plymouth Corinthian Yacht Club was our cruising home for 1996. We were actually based at Mount Batten, which is across the Plymouth Sound from the yacht club, in huge

Cruisers relaxing at SCYC Abersoch

former flying boat hangers. We were able to leave the boats fully rigged with their sails in these enormous buildings. We had trips up the Tamar, past the naval dockyard with its warships, and beyond Brunel's famous railway bridge at Saltash, and the road bridge alongside. We sailed across the bay to Cawsand, where we had Cornish pasties for lunch to celebrate crossing the county line. On a day too breezy for fun we were offered a trip on a motor launch to see a tall ship coming into harbour. We were just behind the Plymouth Bar when the motor launch broke down, so we called on the GP fleet rescue boats who were going past with the returning fleet to give us a hand. It was a fantastic sight to see all the little GPs surrounding the tall ship, and going faster too.

In 1997 the World Championship was held at Skerries Sailing Club in Ireland, so the cruising fleet went there too. It was a most hospitable week as only the Irish can provide. We had a trip to Gormanston Army Camp, where we looked at vintage aeroplanes and lunched in the Officer's Mess (in spite of our wet gear). We visited privately owned Lambay Island, where we had special permission to land, ate our lunch on the golden beach and had a tour of the harbour. And then Loughshinny, where we heard tales of Finn McCool and his daring deeds. A marvellous week, fantastic hospitality, good friendships made and renewed, fun and relaxation. Who wants to race anyway?

It was the MacNationals at Largs in 1998. This is a beautiful place for cruising on the west coast of Scotland, but the most notable feature of our week was the wet and windy weather. Even the sheep wore wellies this year. However we did manage to sail on most days. I suppose sailors are used to getting wet. Our escort boat was the Queen's Harbour Master's 'Barge', a splendid vessel. There was also a little dory ready for the closer action. We circumnavigated Great Cumbrae, calling in at Millport on the south end of the island for the 'must do' visit to the Ritz café for home made ice cream. We picnicked at remote Glencallum Bay on Bute, keeping the boats anchored and wading ashore because of the huge boulders. Our sail to Kilchatton was in light winds and even a little sunshine. On the way, one cruiser was ostensibly fishing, indeed they must have caught something big because one of the crew fell out of the boat! After we squeezed into the little harbour at Kilchatton some cruisers took out their camping stove and prepared hot soup. The MacNationals ended with auld lang syne in the truest sense, with all of us looking forward to renewing acquaintances next time.

For cruising in 1999 it was the estuary at Falmouth in Cornwall, with the racers in the Nationals not far away at Mount's Bay Sailing Club at Marazion. The weather was lovely and sunny all week. The wind however, went from not much, to too much, to virtually none at all. We enjoyed visiting the creeks and crannies of the river Fal. We called in at St Just to see the church, then Trelissick to see the gardens. We went past King Harry Ferry (with only just enough wind) and those enormous ships that are moored in the river by the Smuggler's Cottage, where we had lunch. We even went far enough up river to wave to the Cathedral at Truro. We visited St Mawes, St Anthony's Lighthouse and saw the World War Two gun battery on the headland there. We ventured across the bay to the river Helford, where Daphne du Maurier's Frenchman's Creek didn't look the least bit romantic as it was just low tide mud. We also joined the racers at Mount's Bay for a sherry party and an exclusive tour of St Michael's Mount courtesy of Lord St Leven. It was a great week, full of sunshine with lots of interest, ideal for cruising, especially in a versatile boat like the GP14.

For the year 2000 several weekend cruises are being planned for different venues around the country, following responses to the Association's questionnaire.

Occasionally racers have been overheard to say, "Why is it we bounce around for hours and sail from one buoy to the next, when the cruising fleet sail from pub to pub and walk around with huge grins all the time?" To sum up the differences between racing and cruising, we have a definition of a racer at the Nationals: - one who swears at 900 wind shifts and the consequent postponements. Then we have a definition of a cruiser: - one who just smiles and heads for a different beach for lunch.

Kathy Robinson

Cruisers at Abersoch 'Get More Wind' 1990

'An Old Cruiser'

I guess boats and the sea have always had a fatal fascination for me. Having a brother in the Navy, there was always talk of the sea at home and pictures of ships

Way back (and I mean way-back!) when I was young girl in the Naval Training Corps, we used to team up with the local Sea Cadets and go off for fun weekends on the Norfolk Broads and just enjoy messing about in boats

The first boat I owned was a Heron, I was living in Australia at the time and had friends who used to race Herons every weekend and I used to go and watch.

I returned to the UK around Christmas 1980 and one of the first things I wanted to check out was where the nearest water and sailing club was. This was Whitefriars at Ashton Keynes. In the spring of 1981 I would go up to the club to watch the sailing and meet like-minded friends. That was when I was first introduced to a GP14. What I liked about this boat was the high boom and somewhere to put my long legs. But then you are supposed to be comfortable when sailing, I was told! The boat I eventually bought was one I had watched winning all the races, with trophies to prove it. This was 8784 and named 'Mermerus'. I was informed that this was the name of a famous sailing ship. I was very happy with all this. However, for some reason, 'Mermerus' failed to win anymore races. (I wonder why, different helm perhaps?), I became disenchanted with racing - people get so aggressive and not the nice people I thought they were. However, I did enjoy cruising around.

In 1982 I was on holiday in Brittany and after setting up camp our neighbours invited us to join them for a cup of tea. Imagine our surprise when out came a beautiful silver teapot bearing the inscription of a G.P14 and with the name Simon Relph - I hadn't heard of 'Richard' at that time! These friendly people were Simon's parents in-laws. Such a small world isn't it? Can't wait to go to Carnac!

In 1987 it was announced that Lee-on-the-Solent Sailing Club, in addition to hosting the National Championships, the club would, at the same time be running a GP14 Cruising Week; I was delighted and thought, this is for me. After all, who wants to sit in a boat waiting for the weather to change just to race from A-B, well perhaps a bit further, when you can get moving on the water and enjoy the beauty of the sea and explore the surrounding places of interest, which are often only accessible by boat?

I found the GP14 a great boat to trail - except I find the mast quite a handful to erect and lower. Looking back in Mainsail, winter 1982, I note the owner of GP, 10047 was making the same comment. However, there are usually helpful people around wherever I go. What fun it is looking back in old issues of Mainsail and even more fun looking back at my snapshots taken at all the Nationals and here we are almost back at Mumbles again but sadly, no cruising this time.

Cruising on River Conway 1993

By late 1996, 'Mermerus' needed a lot of maintenance and I was vaguely looking around at other boats. I visited Sailboat 1997 and the Speed Sails stand where 'Richard' charmed me with his sales talk and I lingered long enough looking at the new FRP GP14 to get hooked. In June 1997 I took delivery of GP 13549, now christened 'Opus I' and this boat was a whole new ball game. Could I work out the cascade kicker? It was different every time I rigged the boat. "Richard, remember promising to send me a diagram to follow?" - I'm still waiting! 'Opus 1' made her maiden voyage at Skerries that year.

1998 was at Largs where the cruisers were escorted by the Queen's Harbourmaster's 'Barge' and where my crew, for some reason, decided to leave the boat and I experienced my first capsize. What did Speed Sails' leaflet say about this boat - 'easy to right after a capsize'! Well it beat us. OK Charlie, you did find my spinnaker pole on the beach the next morning and at least we were not stuck in the mud - fellow cruisers will understand!

Falmouth last year was different and one of the best Cruising Weeks, although I say that after every Nationals. Now we have Kit to help us keep the cruisers together and we must organise events for this year. But we mustn't forget Weir Quay, which is always a great Cruising Weekend, thanks to Jenny;

What a lot of enjoyment GP14 has given me and what great friends I have made by belonging to the GP Fourteen Class International Association. But at the end of the day, I guess I am just 'An Old Cruiser'.

Cynthia Papworth
GP13549 'Opus I'

The West Lancashire Yacht Club 24 Hour Race

An event in which the GP14 plays a significant role

One National event in which the GP14 has played a significant part for 30 of its 50 years is the West Lancashire Yacht Club's (WLYC) 24Hour Race. The race, which is synonymous with good sailing and good fun, has drawn GP14 and Enterprise Class sailors from the UK, France and Ireland, up to Southport in September each year to engage in this unique event.

Original idea

The race was conceived in 1966. In the following year the Borough of Southport would be celebrating its centenary and it was asking local organisations to arrange suitable events. Coincidentally, Liverpool University, who were affiliated to WLYC, wanted to organise an invitation university event and proposed a 12 hour event in September, a time when students would be available before the next academic year. However, not wanting to start or finish in the dark, the WLYC sailing committee, knowing that the enclosed shallow waters of the Southport Marine Lake allowed for safe, close quarter sailing in darkness, extended it to 24 hours, and the Southport Centenary 24 Hour Race was born.

West Lancashire 24 Hour Race

The simple principle of the race is the boat that goes the furthest, wins. The boats always sail a triangular course clockwise around the 24 hectares lake. Crew changes are permitted, and no restrictions are placed on the numbers in a team. Whilst the racing is taking place, a vast organisation of mainly WLYC volunteers provide race organisation, resuscitation and recuperation with musical entertainment thrown in; as if the activity on the water were not entertaining enough.

Classes and Clubs

For the first race in 1967 invitations were sent out to all universities and all the sailing clubs in the north west. The interest was overwhelming and 50 boats competed in GP14s, Enterprise and Firefly dinghies. The WLYC team appreciated the sailing logistics a little better than most of the other teams, and had even practiced crew changeovers, but even so were delighted to win the first event.

By 1973 the Fireflys had been withdrawn from the event and up until the mid 1990's the race continued as a handicap event between GP14 and Enterprise dinghies. By 1996 a body of data had been gathered which showed that, for this particular event, neither design of dinghy had an advantage over the other, and therefore the race has been run on par, without PN adjustment since then. By 1999, the number of universities participating had fallen off, partly because they were sailing neither GP14s or Enterprises. Following trials on the lake with the Lark, Laser 2 and RS200 the Lark Class was permitted to compete in the Race, on handicap. Seventy Five boats entered the 1999 event, of which 33 were GP14s, 32 Enterprises and 10 Larks. There were eight university teams. The race was won by Blackpool and Fleetwood YC in a GP14. This was their third success. Equally WLYC have won the event three times, but Bolton Sailing Club have won the race 11 times, between 1970 and 1995.

The Scoring System

Before the first race it was recognised that an efficient scoring and reporting system would be required in order to keep the spectators informed about progress on the water. Pre-computerisation, a mechanical system of a continuous paper stream for each class of boat, driven by differential gearing in accordance with the PN, was used to record each boat as it passed "B" and "D" mark. The distance on the paper represented the adjusted elapsed time, so that it was a straightforward matter to sort the boats into position at each hour and publish the interim positions. By the end of the race the rolls were 30 metres long, but they provided a permanent record of what had transpired in the event of a query.

In later years the scoring system's paper rolls were replaced with model boats 'sailing' around on a large rotating circular table. In theory, as the boat on the water passed 'D' mark, so the boat on the table was level with the 'D mark Puller' who would pull the boat

from the table and pass it to the 'Bonker', who would punch the club's clock card with the time. Simultaneously the club number was entered into a BBC computer which would sort and print the interim positions. As the boat passed 'A' mark it was replaced on the table.

In latter years however, a bank of computers, monitor, check and report on the boats' progress, with the positions even being reported on the Internet every half hour, allowing, in 1999 supporters in Hong Kong to keenly follow the race live.

WLYC has as its primary objective "The encouragement of amateur yacht and boat sailing". Through the establishment and provision of one of the premier events in the dinghy sailing calendar for over 30 years, it has surely satisfied that goal, particularly for members of the GP14 International Class Association.

Kit Robinson
GP14 1850 & 13450

Team Racing

Competition is inevitable whether between individuals or clubs once a sport is established. I do not know the history of Team Racing in dinghies but I guess that it was well established before the war. After all, yacht racing was commonplace in the 19th century.

In the GP14 Class the earliest record of Team Racing is from Royal Windermere Y.C. when on September 14th. 1952, they took part in an event having six visiting teams.

Later in the 50's, meetings were held in October to arrange Open Meetings and Team Racing events. They were held both at Manchester Cruising Association and Midland S.C. All Classes were included and at the end of a busy evening most clubs came away with a full fixture list.

My club, Nantwich was between the north west and midland areas. We had, I remember, some 14 clubs to visit or entertain each year. Add to these the Open Meetings and you have a pretty busy season.

Most racing took place in a borrowed boat, one was never to have the advantage of sailing one's own boat; teams changing boats for each race.

It was a great classroom for rules, tactics and tricks. Rivalry was, if possible, greater when part of a team and many a lesson was learned from the likes of the Price brothers at West Kirby, and Tom Crossley at Northwich. Of course in those days any indiscretion meant a quick return to the shore.

In the early 60's the National GP14 Team Racing Championship was inaugurated at The Welsh Harp by Wembley S.C. They hosted it until 1965 attracting up to 20 teams from all over the country.

The 'dark horse' finalists, of 1965, Red Wharf Bay S.C. hosted the 1966 & 1967 Championships with Holyhead S.C. at Holyhead. Again over 16 teams attended.

Back to England, The Winsford Flash S.C. took on the mantle of host club for a few years.

I have never known why Team Racing lost its charm, for they were the halcyon years for many of us in the Midlands. Visits to other clubs and having your friends 'at home' brought fellowship and variety to our sport.

Team Racing is alive and well as the recent World Championships showed, when West Kirby S.C. hosted the event a few years ago. They were able to demonstrate that it could be an exciting spectator sport even to the uninitiated. Sailed in colourful boats on a small course before a grandstand full of the public and yachtsmen, brought this aspect of the sport to a new peak of entertainment. Let it long be encouraged.

The GP14 Championships have not been in the fixture list since 1996 when it was held at Burwain S.C.

Peter Sandbach

Training Schemes and Plas Menai

Howard-Davies Memorial Youth Training Week, Plas Menai, 1990

From the outset the GP14 has been used for training. Initially owners learnt the hard way, ie. by their mistakes. Largely that was true for the racing rules as well - who said they are still learning, 50 years on?

Many clubs saw the need, often to attract more members, to organise sail training sessions. In the late 50s and 60s there were many Instructor's Courses, using the RYA syllabus and many club sailors obtained their certificates. From this foundation, training courses started in most clubs at the beginning of each season.

The GP was chosen by many sailing schools as an excellent starter boat. For their customers, it is stable, spacious, uncomplicated, and able to take the knocks. It was not always necessary to take three students at a time in the well known alternative. Not only in the UK, but also round the world, many schools use the GP. You will see a row of them each season, by the Swan River at Perth.

Training is not only about on the water activity. From the early days, sailmakers were pleased to come to a club to talk about sail setting - good for business of course. This has continued and some of our present sailmakers are well known round our branches in Africa and Australia as well as the UK. They take the skills a lot further, including rigging and the whole spectrum of boat preparation.

The Association has always been keen to encourage the training of young people. Howard-Davies, after a career in the Merchant Service, dedicated himself to seamanship training of cadets. This was first at the Outward Bound School at Aberdovey then at HMS Conway where he himself had been a cadet. When Howard died in 1998 it seemed appropriate to remember him through the training of young people in the skills of helming and crewing. Not only that but to do it on the water he knew so well, The Menai, North Wales. The Plas Menai National Outdoor Sports Centre, is situated almost opposite the old HMS Conway School, where he had been the sailing instructor.

It was decided that the Association would fund a one week residential course at the school for young sailors who were, through their family or club, associated with the GP. This course, using their own GPs, is held each year in October. It specifically includes crewing, a skill so often ignored. The school instructors take the twelve girls and boys through an advanced racing course on the extremely tidal waters of the Straits, a new experience for many who have previously only known lake sailing. Since its inception, over 100 students have benefited from this course. The Association continues to encourage clubs with their training courses and introduces them to expertise appropriate to their needs.

Exhibitions

The first recorded exhibition where the GP14 was shown was the South Bank Exhibition in 1958. Our records suggest that GP7 was built at this show. Wherever the GP14 was to be found, clubs or owners managed to get it into any show going. Whether it be The London Boat Show or exhibitions in Scotland, Dublin, Melbourne or Perth, the GP was taken to the public.

Bell Woodworking and later Moores of Wroxham found space for us at Earls Court. Members of the London clubs providing Association representatives for very many years. At this show there would be a GP Fourteen Class Association meeting, several hundred attending.

The Midlands Area was one of the big leisure activity growth regions of the country. The Birmingham Post promoted this with a Sailing, Leisure and Caravan Show, firstly at Bingley Hall then at the NEC when it was completed. GP14's have been there in strength whether on our own or club displays.

Sailboat otherwise known as the National Dinghy Exhibition has had several homes. Picketts Lock, Crystal Palace, and lately Alexandra Palace. We have been to all of them. Sailboat is the Class Association's exhibition. Whilst it is for them primarily, to be economically viable it had to attract the boat builders and chandlers. This combination has been a great success and makes a fine start to the sailing season. To quote the MD of one of the largest International boat fittings manufacturers, "It is the finest sailing dinghy exhibition in the World".

We continue to exhibit at shows small and large whenever possible.

Sailboat 1999 - Alexandra Palace

NATIONAL AND WORLD CHAMPIONSHIP VENUES

YEAR	NATIONAL	WORLD	CHAMPIONS	
1952	SHROPSHIRE S.C.		C.H.D.Acland	
1953	NEW QUAY S.C.		H.N.Norbury	
1954	R.WINDERMERE Y.C.		E.Howard-Davies	
1955	HAMBLE RIVER S.C.		E.Howard-Davies	
1956	HOLYHEAD S.C.		C.D.Grace	
1957	BASSENTHWAITE S.C.		R.Atkinson	
1958	PORT OF PLYMOUTH S.A.		I.M.Banner-Mendus	
1959	HOLYHEAD S.C.		J.Tyler	
1960	HOLYHEAD S.C.		M.R.Sills	
1961	THORPE BAY S.C.		I.R.Willis	
1962	R.TORBAY Y.C.		J.Wright	
1963	LLANDUDNO S.C.		M.L.Peek	
1964	THORPE BAY S.C.		A.E.Setford	
1965	HELENSBURGH S.C.		A.B.Allen	
1966	R.TORBAY Y.C.		J.E.Pallot	
1967	LLANDUDNO S.C.	STORMONT Y.C. CANADA	W.Morris	J. Hoad
1968	THORPE BAY S.C.		J.Mc.William	
1969	BALLYHOLME Y.C.		P.Currie	
1970	PLYMOUTH MAYFLOWER S.C.		D.Warden-Owen	
1971	LLANDUDNO S.C.	THORPE BAY S.C. UK	E.Warden-Owen	A.J.W.Read
1972	WHITSTABLE Y.C.		B.Hayes	
1973	HELENSBURGH S.C.		I.R.Willis	
1974	THORPE BAY S.C.		E.Warden-Owen	
1975	LLANDUDNO S.C.	STONE HARBOUR Y.C. USA	R.Lord	T.W.Whisker
1976	MUMBLES Y.C.		E.Warden-Owen	
1977	TROON S.C.	CLONTARF Y & BC. IRELAND	M.Jolleys	I.R.Willis
1978	THORPE BAY S.C.		I.R.Willis	
1979	LLANDUDNO S.C.	MOUNTS BAY S.C. W.AUSTRALIA	R.Estaugh	R.Estaugh
1980	MUMBLES Y.C.		M.Holmes	
1981		TROON S.C.		R.Estaugh
1982	THORPE BAY S.C.		I.Southworth	
1983	HOLYHEAD S.C.	CORINTHIAN Y.C. USA	I.Southworth	I.Southworth/ R.Estaugh
1984	TROON S.C.		N.Marsden	
1985		MUMBLES Y.C. WALES		S.Relph
1986	MOUNT'S BAY S.C.		R.Estaugh	
1987	LLANDUDNO S.C.		R.Estaugh	
1988	LEE ON THE SOLENT S.C.	HOWTH Y.C. IRELAND	I.Southworth	S.Relph
1989	MUMBLES Y.C.		R.Estaugh	
1990	SOUTH CAERNARFON Y.C.		I.Southworth	
1991	HELENSBURGH S.C.	CORINTHIAN Y.C. USA	R.Estaugh	M.Fekkes
1992	MOUNT'S BAY S.C.		R.Estaugh	
1993	LLANDUDNO S.C.		S.Relph	
1994		LEE ON THE SOLENT S.C.		R.Estaugh
1995	BRIXHAM Y.C.		R.Estaugh	
1996	R.PLYMOUTH CORINTHIAN Y.C.		R.Estaugh	
1997	R.NORFOLK & SUFFOLK Y.C.	SKERRIES S.C. IRELAND	R.Estaugh	R.Estaugh
1998	LARGS S.C.		R.Estaugh	
1999	MOUNTS BAY S.C.		R.Estaugh	

GP14 Class History from the Minute Book

DATE	PRINCIPLE DECISIONS
1951	Meeting of members proposed formation of Association. 'Bell' adopted as insignia. 'Bells of Aberdovey'
1952	Discrepancy between Yachting World and Jack Holt plans & boats First AGM. E.Howard-Davies elected Chairman, Representative of each adopting club to form Assoc. Committee. Spinnakers allowed but in abeyance for one season. 1st.Championship to be held at Shropshire SC. Sailcloth specification introduced. 2nd.AGM. Due to success of Championship, Y.W.Editor asked to rescind decision to discourage GP14 racing. 115 registered members. Confirmed adoption of spinnakers but not 1953 Nat. Champs. Applied for affiliation to Royal Yachting Assoc. Rule change to allow shrouds to pass through deck.
1953	Sub Committee to revise rules.
1954	Code Flag 'A' adopted. Association tie adopted. Constitution adopted. Chairman becomes a President. Only members to helm in Championships. All existing Class Certificates invalid on 1st Jan 1955. Boats to be re-measured to new measurement rules.
1955	Self Bailers discussed. AGM. Area Championships introduced sheet horse design optional. National Champions shall wear additional sail emblem. Association Insurance Scheme inaugurated. Publication of first Handbook agreed. Built in buoyancy allowed. First overseas club affiliated, Penang SC.
1956	Recommended builders list. First boats exported to USA. Terylene materials to be considered for sails. AGM. 482 new members total 1050. Constitution amended to allow branches to be formed. 1st.Scottish Area Championship agreed. Buoyancy min.increased to 600lbs. Many other rule amendments. First Management Committee formed.
1957	AGM. 620 new sail numbers in past year. National status blocked by copyright owner. Boats to be of minimum weight before fitting built in buoyancy. Centreboard slot flaps agreed. Rules for Championships to be prepared.
1958	Hull measurement tolerances amended. Membership 2600, 2487 registered boats. Group members join from Nigeria,S.Rhodesia,Canada & Malaya. Association office opened in Llanfair PG, with Mrs.Gwen Davies as assistant to Secretary. Terylene sailcloth approved with price control. Spinnakers to be permitted from January 1961.
1959	N.American Branch formed.
1960	Spinnaker ballot result - Yes, may be used from 1961. No.4000 accepted by HRH Prince Philip. Revised plans valid from January 1961

DATE	PRINCIPLE DECISIONS
1961	1962 National Championship to be over 1 week. Windows allowed in Headsails.
1962	National Team Racing event agreed at Welsh Harp S.A. Report on first Junior Championship at Aberdovey. Regions defined. Branch status granted to S.Africa, Australia & India.
1963	Redraft of boat rules.
1964	'International' Association agreed. Administrative regions agreed. Committee agrees that GRP will be for the good of the Class. Metal masts agreed for overseas branches.
1965	Plug for GRP boats and metal spars agreed. World Championship in 1967 agreed.
1966	GRP Ballot says 'yes'. Bournes of Nottingham given licence to build.
1967	Genoa introduced. Specification of GRP boats agreed. Rule amendments to accommodate GRP & Metal Spars.
1968	Cruising Week at Plymouth agreed. First edition of Mainsail. Editor, Peggy Robinson. Transom scuppers discussed. World Championship Rules formulated. Scuppers rule agreed. Mk.II GRP Thames Marine design agreed.
1969	Mk.II GRP Bourne Plastics design agreed Mr. E. Howard-Davies retires. Highfield lever permitted.
1970	Mr.G.Mainwaring appointed Honorary Secretary. Crystal Palace Conference held. Australian GRP boat reported. Cruising, Mr.Acland asked that this section of membership be represented on Committee.
1970	AGM Irish Branch constitution agreed.
1971	W.Australia to produce Thames Marine MkII GRP. Mandatory window in Genoa.
1972	Class Cert. Dispensation for disabled helms agreed.
1973	Copyright ownership agreed with Yachting World Plans revision introduced.
1974	VAT introduced on boats, equipment and subs. Rule change to allow alternative rudder design.
1975	D.Baker on RYA/CAC working party. Inner coaming rule amended. Hon.Life Membership for D.Bechtel.
1976	Conditional dispensation for K&P boats. Class Certificate rule amended. Metrication agreed.